COURAGEOUS **PARENTS**
CONFIDENT **KIDS**

COURAGEOUS
PARENTS
CONFIDENT
KIDS

LETTING GO SO YOU BOTH CAN GROW

EDITED BY

Amy Tiemann, Ph.D.

spark press

Chapel Hill

Courageous Parents, Confident Kids – Letting Go So You Both Can Grow

Copyright © 2010 by Amy Tiemann, Ph.D.

Published by Spark Press
1289 North Fordham Boulevard, Suite 333
Chapel Hill, NC 27514
(919) 747-3771
www.MojoMom.com
www.CourageousParents.com

Free Bonus: Top 10 Courage Boosters! Go to www.BothCanGrow.com

ISBN 978-0-9764980-3-2

First printing

This book is intended to be informational and should not be considered a substitute for advice from medical, mental health, financial, or legal professionals. The contributors, editor, and publisher are not responsible for errors, omissions, or inconsistencies herein.

Rather than indicating every occurrence of a trademarked name as such, this book uses the names only in an editorial fashion with no intention of infringement of the trademark.

Cover design by Kathi Dunn, Dunn + Associates Design,
    www.dunn-design.com
Cover illustration by Jane Mjølsness,
    www.janemjolsness.com
Book interior by Dorie McClelland, Spring Book Design,
    www.springbookdesign.com

"Mojo Mom" and "Spark Press" are registered trademarks of Spark Productions, LLC.

The most beautiful sight in the world
is a little child going confidently down
the road of life after you have shown
him the way. ～ Proverb

Contents

Introduction

Amy Tiemann, Ph.D.

Amy Tiemann, Ph.D., is a multimedia producer, educator, and catalyst for social change. She is the celebrated author of *Mojo Mom: Nurturing Your Self While Raising a Family* and founder of the popular online resource MojoMom.com. She reaches a global audience through her writing, podcasts, and media coverage. Tiemann collaborates with the contributors to this book to lead the way to a new era of empowered parenting, based on creativity, connection, and action. She has served on the Executive Team of MomsRising.org, and currently teaches personal safety skills as Center Director of Kidpower North Carolina. Learn more about Amy at www.MojoMom.com.

YOU OUGHTA KNOW . . .

As we turned the calendar page to 2010, a decade of fear and anxiety came to a close. In the decade retrospectives, 2000–2009 is being labeled the "Aughts." This seems perfectly suited to the decade of overparenting, when we were told again and again in so many ways that "you ought to do this" and "you ought not to do that" in order to be a good parent.

This decade also happened to coincide with my daughter's first ten years of life. I became a mother in late 1999, and I have enjoyed this decade of family life so much. Yet, however wonderful our personal experiences may have been over the last ten years, on a larger scale, it has been a tough time to be a parent.

As I look back to my own childhood, I know that the "oughts" and anxieties of parenthood are not new. When I was growing up, missing children's faces were on milk cartons and the spectre of all-out nuclear war was a lurking fear that haunted all of us.

But the bombardment of fearful messages in the media and the marketplace seems to have escalated tremendously in recent years. The media score higher ratings with scary stories than they do with hopeful ones. Marketers pitch us new problems and are right there to sell us the solutions.

The baby-industrial complex has exploded into a trillion-dollar "mom market" of products and services, many of which are unnecessary. For example, many parents were "sold" on Baby Einstein videos that promised to make their infants smarter. The company, which was acquired by Disney in 2001, continues to peddle hundreds of millions worth of baby media products each year even though researchers debunked the concept of creating baby geniuses through these videos in 2007. In response to the research findings and a complaint filed with the Federal Trade Commission, Baby Einstein and other infant media companies have scaled back aggressive marketing messages, such as this claim from Baby Einstein's 1997 product launch press release that was posted on its Web site for years: "Through exposure to phonemes in seven languages, Baby Einstein contributes to increased brain capacity." But as Po Bronson and Ashley Merryman pointed out on their *NurtureShock* blog for *Newsweek,* Disney could afford to dial back its marketing "because it still benefits from the suggestive power of the brand – from the false claims made long ago."

In my opinion, the absolute apex of crazy gadgets can be found in the BabyPlus Prenatal Education System, a $149 ticking pod women are supposed to strap to their pregnant bellies in order to, theoretically, teach their fetuses to recognize sound patterns, giving them the earliest possible head start on learning. A print ad for the BabyPlus system emphasizes a feeling of control and a certainty of good outcomes. The copy, accompanying a photo of a serene pregnant woman, reads, "I know it's a boy. I know his name is Ryan. I know he'll be calmer, happier and brighter because of BabyPlus." This advertisement was run in *Fit Pregnancy*, and BabyPlus mentions continue to occur in other mainstream publications. The gadget is still on the market and even showed up at the 2010 Consumer Electronics Show.

The BabyPlus system is a prime example of how gadgets are often packaged with unrealistic expectations about how much control we can have over the whole enterprise of raising kids, setting up new parents for burnout and disappointment later on. It is more comforting to believe that we call the shots, control life, and can guarantee good health, happiness, and wealth for everyone in our family. Unfortunately, despite our very human tendency to believe otherwise, this is not really how life works. Parenting will teach us to make peace with chaos and unpredictability like no other experience, and it takes courage to face the truth that we can't control everything. It pains me to see baby product sales pitches reinforce our illusions of complete control.

BabyPlus is not only based on a dubious concept, it also seems like the earliest possible mom-leash, teaching women that from the day they conceive they are supposed to devote themselves to their growing embryos even at their own great discomfort or inconvenience. While parenthood does require tons of devotion, investment, and self-sacrifice, I shudder to think of women literally tethering themselves to an unrealistic standard of maternal accommodation even before their children are born. In so many cases, what we naturally have to offer is good enough, without adopting practices that are intrusive and expensive!

The pressure to be a "perfect" parent, regardless of personal or financial cost, is not limited to specialty products like Baby-Plus. When I became pregnant in 1999, the baby-guide bible, *What to Expect When You're Expecting*, still dispensed the advice that a pregnant woman should ponder each bite of food before ingesting it, asking herself, "Is this the best bite I can give my baby?" while following the prescribed "Best Odds Diet," which was supposed to give women the best chance of having a healthy pregnancy and baby. Like many expectant mothers, I was convinced by the book's nagging tone that I was on track to become a slacker mom even before giving birth. Not following the Best Odds Diet felt as irresponsible as turning down an opportunity to purchase a winning lottery ticket. However, after becoming anxious about the frankly unrealistic standards that advised: "If it will benefit your baby, chew away. If it'll only benefit your sweet tooth or appease your appetite, put your fork down" and reading about every strange thing that could go wrong during pregnancy, I finally decided to consult the book only as needed rather than reading it straight-through. While opinion on *What to Expect* is still divided, some of the most strident parts of the text have mellowed out in later editions as the authors decided to drop some of their more controversial recommendations, including the Best Odds Diet.

THE PAST DECADE REALLY WAS SCARY

From terror, to war, to financial meltdown, when we look back over the past ten years, it's not surprising that we were caught up in waves of anxiety, because the decade really *was* scary. Any

American who was old enough on September 11, 2001, to be conscious of what was going on will tell you that life changed that day. The attacks on the World Trade Center, in particular, expanded our notion of what kind of violence was possible in America. The events were truly mind-boggling. That day, by the time I turned on the television, the first tower had already fallen, but the scene was obscured by intense black smoke. Even as the reporters on the television and my husband on the telephone were saying that one tower had fallen, my mind could not wrap itself around that concept. I was hoping the smoke would clear enough to see how damaged the World Trade Center was. It was only when I saw the horrible sight of the second tower crumbling on live TV that I understood the absolute destruction of the entire complex.

On that day, we were understandably riveted by the unfolding news announcing thousands of deaths, an unknown number of looming potential threats, planes crashing into the Pentagon and Pennsylvania, and the grounding of all airplane flights in the United States. I remember shaking off the spell of the news long enough to look over at my daughter, then a toddler, to see what she was doing. Without me even noticing, she had taken apart an entire box of Band-Aids and stuck the pieces all over the carpet right next to me.

The fear of that day shook us to the core and was channeled into persuasive, if dubious, arguments in favor of war. In the past decade, we've lived in a heightened state of anxiety, and it is time for us to look consciously at our patterns of attention and worry.

ANXIETY CAN DISTRACT US FROM WHAT IS REALLY IMPORTANT

It may seem strange to segue from overhyped baby gadgets and books to 9/11, but it all mixes together into our fear diet, which we are fed mostly by the media. Now I will grant that on 9/11 the news of the day justifiably scared the heck out of us – it was a terrifying time. But how about the three thousand days since then? How many fearful headlines are deserved, as opposed to merely being sensationalist bait to get us to watch, read, or click through them? With 24-hour cable news and the Internet's own hyperactive news cycle, every media outlet is competing harder for our attention. Bad news is shown in a persistent, repetitive loop. Stories that are sensationalistic, such as the relatively rare abduction and murder of young women, receive a disproportionate amount of coverage while much more common, equally tragic stories are overlooked. This phenomenon has even spawned the term *missing white woman syndrome,* itself a critique of the fact that similar crimes against people of color are routinely not given the same level of news coverage. Violent crime is a true tragedy for the victims, their loved ones, and their community. However, for the general public, hyperbolic media coverage unnecessarily increases the psychological impact of these terrible – but rare – events, perpetuating a sense of despair and hopelessness that does not honor the victims and does not make anyone safer.

I understand the power of these crimes to evoke both a parent's greatest fears and protective instincts. But we must have the courage to move past our instinctual fears to construct an effective response to such possibilities. Our cultural construction of "Stranger Danger" provides a case in point: we have learned over recent decades that stranger abductions are actually quite rare, yet parents are still disproportionately anxious about "Stranger Danger." This has caused several problems. First, parents distracted by this stereotypical worry are not adequately prepared to address the fact that the vast majority of child abuse is perpetrated by people known to the family, not strangers. Second, parents' paranoia about abduction may result in the unnecessary restriction of children's opportunities to explore the world, depriving them of joyful experiences and the ability to learn the tools they need to develop independence safely.

A 2007 British study demonstrated how children's right to roam has almost disappeared in four generations: an eight-year-old in 1926 who walked six miles without adult supervision to visit his favorite fishing spot is contrasted with his eight-year-old great-grandson who "is driven the few minutes to school, is taken by car to a safe place to ride his bike, and can roam no more than three hundred yards from home." The author of the report, Dr. William Bird, believes this isolation and deprivation of the natural world puts kids' physical and mental health at risk. I also wonder how kids without the opportunity to socialize and gain life experience through free play and exploration fare on their own when it is time to leave the nest.

When so many kids become so restricted, a social problem develops that is bigger than any one family. When kids' peers are not allowed to play outside, every child's isolation increases, because even those children who are granted more freedom are forced to socialize through organized activities. Furthermore, as more parents drive kids everywhere they go, there are increased traffic hazards for those kids who still want to walk. As much as twenty to thirty percent of morning traffic is generated by parents driving their children to school. In the final analysis, due to lack of company and more road traffic, it might be too dangerous to walk to school *because* no one else is doing it! Fortunately, communities across the country are working to reverse this trend by implementing "Safe Routes to School" initiatives.

GROUNDING "HELICOPTER" PARENTING

Educators and even parents themselves are starting to examine the problems that result from curtailed childhood freedoms and over-involved, intrusive helicopter parenting that occurs when Mom and Dad hover over their kids' lives and swoop in to intervene at a moment's notice, even when their "child" is a teen or college student. Some college educators note that the majority of their students' parents are involved in some kind of helicoptering behavior; a recent study showed that first-year college students are more stressed out than ever and are having a hard time coping with their independence.

A close relationship with our kids is a gift, but whose needs are being served when we don't let our young adult children grow up and away? An essential, painful truth of parenthood is that our ultimate job is to make ourselves "unnecessary" – at least in our immediate supervisory role. Are we parents crippling our grown children in a quest to satisfy our own need for closeness, or to stroke our own egos as we live through their accomplishments? In the second installment of a post titled "When Does Mothering Become Smothering?" on Susan Newman's *Psychology Today* blog, parenting writer Adele Faber points out that "the desire to be needed is very powerful in parents. To go from that all-powerful parent whose kids desperately need you to someone who sees a child as a separate individual is a very hard journey."

Fortunately, a new trend is emerging as parents are beginning to wake up to the problems caused by overly intrusive parenting. Indeed, several recent books follow this theme, including *The Price of Privilege* by Madeline Levine, *Under Pressure* by Carl Honore (father of "slow parenting"), *A Nation of Wimps* by Hara Estroff Marano, and *The Parents We Mean to Be* by Richard Weissbourd.

But perhaps the best-known writer in this area is Lenore

Skenazy, who is leading a revolution that she has dubbed the "Free-Range Kids" movement. After Lenore granted her nine-year-old son's request to ride the subway home alone in New York City, she was criticized left and right for being an irresponsible parent. I believe there is room for debate about the wisdom of her decision to let her son ride the subway alone; even so, I was still amazed by the media firestorm that erupted and dubbed Lenore "America's Worst Mom." This reaction shows how easily parents' buttons can be pushed on these issues and how primed we are to react – and sometimes overreact. Fortunately, Lenore responded with grace, good humor, and wickedly incisive writing. She called out overprotective parenting practices that prevent kids from playing or acquiring independence, such as rules that prohibit kids from walking to school or riding bikes to soccer practice, even when parents have judged their kids perfectly capable of doing so. Her *Free-Range Kids* blog and book have become important cultural touchstones, as Skenazy keeps her finger on the pulse of the movement by posting relevant news stories and commentary.

Across the country, parents are starting to take a fresh look at the goal of raising capable, competent, *independent* young adults. The question becomes, Where do we want to go from here, and how do we get there?

THE HEART OF COURAGEOUS PARENTING

To shed our overprotective parenting ways, we have to become conscious of what truly serves our kids' needs and develop the courage to put aside some of the things that may feel good to us as parents but don't serve our children well in the long run. Right now my daughter is ten years old, and I just love this age. I find myself wishing that I could wave a magic wand and freeze-frame my family at this stage for about three more years. It's all going too fast for me! But that's my wish, not her need. She needs her parents to stay with her in the moment, enjoying her as she changes and letting her grow up. When we reach that moment of truth when she's ready to leave home as a young adult, I will try my best to smile when we say goodbye, even if I feel tears welling up inside.

That's where courage comes in – the courage to let our kids grow up and eventually away from us as our role evolves from parental "boss," to "consultant," to respectful adult peer. A close relationship with our kids is wonderful, but we have to keep sight of the big picture: they need to become independent people. This does not happen overnight – they won't magically wake up at age 18, all of a sudden ready to face the world. Independence in adulthood is the result of a thousand little steps along the way. I think of the tiny steps my daughter has already taken or will be taking: getting dressed and tying her own shoes, walking into school on her own, facing new situations and making new friends, resolving disputes with her friends without our intervention, learning household skills like cooking and cleaning, developing the good judgment needed to navigate sleepover parties or summer camp, going on dates, applying for an after-school job. . . . With each step, the balance of power and decision making tips more in her favor until one day she holds the keys not only to the car, but to her own future.

LETTING GO SO YOU BOTH CAN GROW

In the first section of *Courageous Parents, Confident Kids,* we will explore ways that parents can develop their own lives through self-care and lifelong career creation. It is essential for us to continue to cultivate our own identities beyond our roles as parents so that when our kids leave the nest they know that we have full lives to turn to and won't crumple into empty shells once they are gone. Developing our own identities is good for our parenting and it is good for us as individuals – we deserve it.

In the second section, we will move on to talk about several ways that moms and dads can develop their own parenting styles over time. The goal is to eventually each become our own parenting experts, gaining enough experience along the way to feel confident that we are making the best decisions we can for our families. We will talk about easing the free-floating worry we so often feel and lessening its toxic effects so we can focus our attention and energy on the things that we can positively impact. This can be difficult, and it takes courage to let go of the somewhat magical talisman of worry – oftentimes we think active worry can somehow protect our family, as if gripping the armrest of our airplane seat will keep the flight aloft. While parenting needs our thoughtful attention, free-floating worry and anxiety just serve to wear us down and can even prevent us from being truly aware of what is going on around us.

When I see intrusive parental hovering that is more interfering than helpful, I wish that those parents would bottle some of that energy and redirect it toward solving the social problems that families face in the United States, where we still have not enacted the kind of family-friendly policies enjoyed in most other parts of the world. In the final section, we will explore this issue in depth, learning how parents have found their political voices, joined together in communities for personal support as well as social action, and in the case of MomsRising.org, harnessed this energy into a massive grassroots campaign that advocates for family-positive policies such as paid parental leave, health care for all families, and protection for mothers against job discrimination.

SKILLS, THE MISSING INGREDIENT!

Courageous Parents, Confident Kids has a key theme: a focus on skills. Taking a step back from overparenting does *not* mean being an inattentive parent. Through the expertise of the anthology contributors, we will run the gamut from honing our parenting skills to developing our "letting-go" skills, learning along the way how to teach our kids the skills *they* need to succeed in each new step they take toward independence. This skill-building theme is woven through the whole book, but the third section focuses specifically on the skills necessary for kids to experience their independence *safely*. Kidpower founder Irene van der Zande writes about personal safety skills that empower kids to explore the real world with confidence. Internet safety expert Linda Criddle addresses online safety and outlines a skill-building process the entire family can go through so that we parents can feel comfortable saying *yes* to our kids' online activities.

This focus on skills is really important to me. Some of the other discussions about the end of overparenting have shied away from this angle. As Nancy Gibbs wrote in her November 2009 *Time* magazine cover story on the topic, "The revolutionary leaders are careful about offering too much advice. Parents have gotten plenty of that, and one of the goals of this new movement is to give parents permission to disagree or at least follow different roads." I agree that parents should feel free to explore different paths and ultimately develop a parenting style that suits them, and it is true that there is no one answer that applies to every family and situation. I also feel strongly that if we as parents want to explore new options, we have to discuss what a new path might look like, where it might lead, and what steps we can take to get there. So far, the movement away from overparenting has been successful in motivating parents to consider a new direction. The goal of this anthology is to expand the conversation by exploring what it means to be courageous, what qualities we can develop in ourselves, and what concrete skills we need to know in order to teach our kids to be independent. We also explore the themes of personal and professional development, the power of speaking up, and the importance of an active, caring community.

As the editor and publisher of *Courageous Parents, Confident Kids*, I invited each of the contributing authors because she had an area of knowledge and experience that I thought was important to share with a wide audience. I have spent years developing relationships with these talented experts. Each and every one of them has changed my life in a significant way, and they have the potential to do so for you, too!

While the contributors to this book are writing on a common theme, each is writing from her own point of view, and like any opinionated group of people, they are not necessarily always in complete agreement with each other, or with me. It is up to you to decide how to customize and apply this information to your life. Writing a book is a bit like scattering seeds of information – one can't predict which ideas will take root and grow in the minds of individual readers. To me, this is part of the fun of sharing new ideas.

An anthology is a snapshot of a continuing conversation, and we intend to keep this dialogue going online in ways that involve both mothers and fathers. It is worth mentioning that I also invited several men to write for this anthology, but scheduling conflicts and prior commitments meant that they were not able to contribute chapters to this book. In the future, I hope to find new ways to share their stories and expertise.

On my Web site, MojoMom.com, you'll find a page dedicated to *Courageous Parents, Confident Kids*. You can also catch up on my latest news and commentary through my blog, and you can listen to *Mojo Mom Podcast* interviews with each of the contributors to this book, as well as other kindred spirits, including authors Lenore Skenazy of *Free-Range Kids*, Marc and Amy Vachon of *Equally Shared Parenting*, Karen Maezen Miller of *Momma Zen* and *Hand Wash Cold*, and Dr. Michele Borba of *The Big Book of Parenting Solutions*.

This anthology is the third book I have had the privilege to work on, and all three have ultimately shared the same theme: *enjoy the journey.* On behalf of all our contributors, this is our *Courageous Parents, Confident Kids* wish for you!

section one

The Courage to Invest in Your Own Development

Why does a book about "Courageous Parents" start with an exploration of a parent's own self-development? I firmly believe that self-care, along with personal and professional development, builds a necessary foundation that empowers parents to raise independent kids. There are so many notions about self-sacrifice built into our cultural notions of parenthood – particularly motherhood – and these ideas generally do not serve us well. When mothers are expected to devote every ounce of energy and dedication to their kids at the expense of all other areas of their lives, the stage is set for overparenting. We can become both personally depleted and overly invested in our kids in a way that is not healthy for anyone. Parents deserve to set aside time and energy for themselves. After all, we are in this for the long run.

"Sustainability" is a vital concept for the whole planet right now, and I believe that sustainability begins at home: within ourselves, our approach to parenting, and our family lives. This can start with basic needs; for instance, some parents overlook their own nutrition, sleep, and basic medical care in ways that they would never neglect their kids'. Or, parents let their batteries run down by overcommitting themselves to their children, partners, friends, and communities – an unhealthy practice that is difficult to continue long-term. Yet all around us we see parents who are doing just that. It takes courage to buck the trend and refuse to join these parents in leading completely overwhelming lives. Instead, we can take stock of our priorities and consciously select meaningful and realistic goals rather than taking on every possible responsibility and activity.

When I encounter helicopter parents of teens, I see both young adults who have not been taught how to fight their own battles, and parents who are unwilling to let go. The empty nest can be both a liberating and frightening prospect for many parents – I know it is for me, even though it looms many years down the road. But one of the greatest gifts we can give our children is to live in a way that makes it clear to them that we will be okay after they leave, and that we fully support their growing autonomy.

No matter where each of us is on our parenting journey, we can begin preparing for our kids' independence (as well as our own) *right now.* The great news is that doing so can actually involve pleasure rather than pain! In this section, Renee Peterson Trudeau gets us started with her practical exploration of how to cultivate "The Transformative Power of Self-care." In my work as "Mojo Mom," I have seen what a challenge it is for parents, especially mothers, to create the self-care foundation that we need to remain happy and healthy in the long run. Taking good care of ourselves and maintaining our individual identity is a necessity, not a luxury: when parents get burned out, it creates a real problem for the whole family. (Or, as we say here in the South, "When Mama ain't happy, ain't *nobody* happy.") Renee's work has helped thousands of women explore and give voice to what they really need, and her Personal Renewal Group trainings have enabled women to create support circles in their own communities.

A lifelong career path is another important part of a parent's identity, as well as a key component of a family's ongoing financial support. Workplace flexibility experts Kella Hatcher and Maryanne Perrin explore ways to carve out a career path that is in harmony with your parenting responsibilities *and* your professional goals. As hard as it may be to imagine when our kids are young, it is worth remembering that many of us will experience *more years of life with our children living away from the nest than we did with them living at home.* Again, here we need to plan for long-term sustainability – both in terms of finances and family life. Few of us can afford to ignore our lifelong earning potential, and in "Tools for Career Reinvention," Kella and Maryanne provide strategies for career development that are more flexible than a traditional, rigid career ladder.

Currently, the workforce is in transition due to new social trends (that the workplace has not caught up with yet) and new ways of working made possible by modern technology. Women are now more than half of the workforce in the United States, but jobs are still often structured for the ideally "unencumbered" male. We are caught between traditional 9-to-5 work structures and a modernized way of working that can be more decentralized, mobile, and focused on results, rather than on punching clocks or logging face time. In the meantime, it can be frustrating to feel that we are stuck with a half-evolved system that often does not acknowledge workers' family responsibilities. Kella and Maryanne firmly believe that workplace transformation is coming, especially since the influential Baby Boomers are reaching retirement age but often are looking for nontraditional alternatives to full-stop retirement. Boomers are also grappling with the reality of caring for their own aging parents or spouses. Caregiving ultimately affects everyone, and we can be pioneers in asking our employers to support us as parents and families.

The Transformative Power of Self-care

Renee Peterson Trudeau

Life balance and career coach and speaker Renee Peterson Trudeau is the author of *The Mother's Guide to Self-Renewal: How to Reclaim, Rejuvenate and Re-Balance Your Life*, which provided the foundation for this chapter. Thousands of women around the globe are joining or becoming trained to lead Personal Renewal Groups (PRGs) using the *Guide*. Trudeau encourages all women to "find their tribe," whether that is through one of the hundreds of Personal Renewal Groups meeting worldwide or another women's circle. Learn more about PRGs, retreats, coaching, and life balance resources at www.ReneeTrudeau.com.

The life I desire is marked by deep connections to my child and partner. It's a life filled with joy and meaning. It's a life in which I feel supported and nurtured by an incredible community of men and women – young and old. I experience regular, meaningful, heartfelt connections with people I care about. I am continually open to growth – as a woman, a mother, a partner, and a spiritual being. I enjoy supporting and serving others in a way that feeds me rather than drains me. I feel that I always have enough time in my life for those things that are most important to me. My life flows, I trust my intuition, and I expect good to come to me. I feel peaceful. I am loving, and I feel loved. This is the life I desire.

It was only after I became a mother and truly connected to my needs and desires that I was finally able to articulate this.

Growing up as the oldest of seven children – five boys and two girls – I remember breakfast at our house being extremely hectic.

My harried mom was scrambling to make lunches, my dad was running around looking for tennis shoes, and invariably one of the seven of us was in the kitchen cooking peanut butter oatmeal, rice-flour pineapple muffins, or some other strange concoction. In our family, we were heartily encouraged to master life skills; this philosophy encouraged lots of cooking experiments but invariably led to mayhem in the kitchen!

One morning, my nine-year-old brother, Kert, now a macrobiotic chef, decided to make some pecan waffles. As I reached over the waffle maker to help myself to breakfast, I bumped the edge of the hot grill and burned my elbow. I must have been ten years old at the time.

I didn't mention the accident to my parents – probably because they seemed too distracted getting my siblings out the door to school – but hours later, I was sitting in my classroom at school, trying to ignore the pain from a small, brown, bubbly-looking burn on my elbow.

Rather than go to a teacher for help or a bandage, I simply endured the discomfort, thinking, *it's not really important enough to bother anyone. I'll be fine.*

This is my earliest recollection of ignoring my basic needs – self-care was not something that was promoted or honored in my family even though my parents were medical professionals! It was definitely something I had to learn on my own.

SELF-CARE: BEYOND MASSAGES AND PEDICURES

When women think about self-care, often visions of pedicures and facials come to mind.

Physical self-care is a big part of the overall picture. But eliminating self-critical thinking, not over-scheduling, releasing the need to be perfect, saying no, refusing to do things out of guilt, and giving yourself much-needed rest and downtime to refuel are also integral to total self-care.

Self-care is about nurturing yourself on all levels – physically, mentally, emotionally, and spiritually – so you can live, love, and parent optimally.

My friend Megan, mom to Mateo, three, and Alea, one, shared how frustrated she was feeling recently. Exhausted from staying up until two a.m. the night before to do laundry, she had skipped breakfast and lunch, was surviving on nothing but coffee, and had been beating herself up all day about not getting a homemade meal over to her neighbor, who had recently lost her father.

As she and I visited, it dawned on us that we would never imagine denying our children sleep or nourishment, being judgmental of them, or allowing them to ignore their emotional needs. Yet, as mothers, we do this to ourselves on a daily basis.

The same love, gentle care, and compassion we offer so generously to our little ones should be extended to ourselves as well. Regardless of what we tell our children about honoring one's own value, we teach them about self-worth through our actions, not our words. Child development experts tell us that modeling self-love and self-acceptance is the most effective way to influence a child's self-esteem and how they view themselves.

Listed below you'll find several examples of ideas for how you can begin nurturing yourself and start making self-renewal part of your everyday life. Depending on the age of your children and your life stage, the activities that interest you may vary greatly.

(Many moms with infants know that even taking a shower or going to the bathroom when you need to are forms of self-care when you're caring for an new baby!)

Try focusing on one area of self-care at a time; which one is calling to you right now?

Physical Care Examples

Nourish your body by eating healthy and energizing foods that make you feel great

Get enough sleep, take naps, and drink plenty of water to stay hydrated

Exercise to replenish your energy and manage stress

Take time to enjoy and nurture your body: take a hot aromatherapy bath or give yourself a foot massage

Emotional Care Examples

Have a heart-to-heart with a close friend or mentor

Have kind and loving thoughts about yourself: try not criticizing yourself for one week

Seek out support from a therapist, coach, social worker, or counselor

Write down your feelings and thoughts in a journal

Go on a fun date alone or with your partner or organize a monthly girls' night out

Spiritual Care Examples

Take time to be by yourself to think or write

Take a walk in a park or out in nature

Meditate, pray, or just reflect on what you're grateful for

Do something creative: paint, draw, write, dance, or sing

Volunteer for a cause you're passionate about

Mental Care Examples

Read a good book or see an intellectually stimulating movie

Learn a new hobby or skill

Sign up for a class, group, or workshop on a topic that
  interests you

Challenge yourself to learn something new – get out of
  your comfort zone

BARRIERS TO SELF-CARE

Almost any mother can share with you how pervasive ideals such as *good mothers always put their families first, motherhood is pure bliss, you just have to let your body go when you become a mom,* or *good mothers are completely selfless,* abound in our society.

These beliefs run deep – even if we don't buy-in to them on a conscious level – and can have a profound impact on how we view our roles as women and mothers. Realize this and be aware that the concept of self-care may feel foreign and difficult to embrace at first, to say the least!

One evening, while facilitating a Personal Renewal Group (PRG) – a self-renewal circle for mothers based on my book, *The Mother's Guide to Self-Renewal: How to Reclaim, Rejuvenate and Re-Balance Your Life* – I asked the women to voice what they perceived the barriers to self-care to be.

This is what they shared: they were afraid others would think they were selfish or otherwise bad moms if they put their needs first; they felt they shouldn't really need self-care; they wouldn't have time for self-care activities or the activities would be too expensive; they had a hard time seeing the value, and regardless of the benefits of self-care, it felt like just one more thing to add to their to-do list; and last, but most important, they held an underlying belief that they were not worthy of self-care. They felt that they didn't deserve to make their needs a priority.

My experience in working with thousands of women through Personal Renewal Groups – which focus on self-care and reconnecting with who you are – is that to successfully implement a self-care practice, you have to dig deep and ask yourself, *What is my personal motivation for self-care?*

The answer will be different for each of us. But if you truly want to experience a shift in your behavior and perspective, the motivation has to come from the inside out. For many women, prioritizing self-care is radical; and for most, it is counter to a culture that doesn't reward or value women putting their needs first.

Most of us can wrap our minds around the idea that self-care makes good sense. We understand its importance on an intellectual level. But for real change to take place, you have to pause, engage your heart, and ask yourself, *Why does this really matter to me, and how might this positively impact my relationships with my family?*

WHY SELF-CARE?

What are some reasons that self-care is important, and how do we benefit by making time for it?

- By filling our cups first, we tend to feel more generous and can avoid building resentments toward others who demand our energy and time.

- Making our self-care a priority is one of the best ways to validate and honor our own worth, which in turn enhances true confidence and self-esteem.

- Taking care of ourselves on all levels – physically, mentally, emotionally, spiritually – helps us feel alive and whole, so we are able to function at our best and do all the things we want to do.

- By taking time to care for ourselves, we renew and restore our energy supply and create energy reserves so we're able to weather unforeseen challenges more easily.

- Practicing self-care and being loving and gentle toward ourselves helps us to be more present and calm, so we can respond wisely, intuitively, and effectively to a variety of circumstances.

- Owning our personal power (realizing our potential) is our birthright; self-care, self-love, and self-acceptance are effective avenues for reaching this goal.

- Nurturing ourselves makes us feel more loving and playful, which makes us better friends, partners, and parents and more fun to be around!

- Nurturing our essence, both inside and out, promotes overall well-being and a sense of vitality.

The journey to making self-care a priority and understanding how life-altering it can be is an evolutionary process. It takes time. As the women in my Personal Renewal Group shared that evening, most people will initially equate self-care with selfishness. Therefore, a huge paradigm shift is needed to make it an everyday practice.

Having grown up with a mother who suffered from depression and struggled constantly with low self-worth and self-esteem, I am motivated to make self-care an important part of my life so I can model this behavior for my son. I want him to see the value of practicing self-care and how it can positively impact how he feels about himself and others.

One afternoon, my seven-year-old son called out to me from his bedroom, "Come play with me, Mom."

I paused for a minute as I walked out of my office and stopped at his doorway. "Not right now, sweetie. I had a really hard day and need to take a few minutes for myself before we begin making dinner." As I headed to my room to rest for a few minutes, I thought about the wonderful quote from Audrey Lorde, author, cancer survivor, and marathon athlete: "Caring for myself is not self-indulgence, it is self-preservation . . ."

I smiled thinking how attuned my son will be as an adult, I hoped, to how essential self-care is for us all. Not only for the women in his life now and in the future, but for himself, as well.

HOW SELF-CARE AFFECTS OUR PARENTING

One of the biggest benefits of a self-care practice is that it supports us in being more present with our partner and children. When we're present with those around us, we're able to experience openness, connection, joy, playfulness, spontaneity, compassion, empathy, gratitude, wisdom, and enhanced communication.

In *Slowing Down to the Speed of Life*, authors Richard Carlson and Joseph Bailey share the several serious consequences that follow when your tank is empty, you're out of sync with your needs, and you're engaging in busy-minded, speeded-up parenting. Some of them include:

> You become habitually reactive instead of responsive
>
> You take negative behavior personally rather than seeing the innocence
>
> [You allow] little events [to] become front-page news
>
> You miss [out on] the good times
>
> You lose sight of your compassion
>
> You expect too much from your children

We live in a 24/7 culture that is overly focused on multitasking and producing. Most of us were never taught that *being* is just as important as *doing*. Slowing down and cultivating an appreciation of just being is not something most of us learned. It's a new orientation. Ultimately, I believe the lesson is to teach our kids that we value them for *who they are* over *what they do*.

Becoming attuned to your needs and what feeds you and creating space to nurture yourself doesn't happen overnight. But after you taste the benefits of focusing on your self-care, you'll begin to see how big the payoffs are. And, eventually, you'll begin to schedule time for self-nurturing just like you schedule doctor or dentist appointments. You'll discover that it is integral to your emotional survival and that you are wiser and more effective in all areas of your life when you take time to fill your cup first.

"The other night at dinner my husband commented on how much more relaxed and joyful I seemed since I had started exercising and taking 'journaling dates,'" shares Ella, a Personal Renewal Group member in Chicago, self-employed writer, and mom to twins. "And, since I started taking time for me, I also feel more generous and playful with my kids. I'm definitely more in touch with my needs."

The changes she made in her life inspired her husband to focus on his self-care, and now he takes guitar classes every Wednesday night. Ella uses that evening to connect with other moms whose partners also claim Wednesday night for their solo dates. The women have dubbed these regular dinners out with the kids as the "Wednesday Night Widows' Club," and all involved look forward to and relish these weekly community gatherings.

For many of us, the most powerful self-care stand we'll ever take is to cultivate self-acceptance and when needed, practice "good is good enough" parenting.

As a recovering perfectionist and control freak, I slowly came to realize that working on releasing self-critical thoughts and easing my unreasonably high expectations of myself – particularly regarding parenting and motherhood – was the kindest self-care action I could take.

When my friend Andrea shared with her mother-in-law, Sally, what she was working on in her Personal Renewal Group – taking time for self-renewal and reconnecting with her desires and needs – Sally's eyes welled up with tears. She told Andrea, "I wish I had taken time for myself when I was raising my boys. Honestly, I just felt so overwhelmed by all the crazy expectations I placed on myself during that time, it was hard for me to focus on much else. Because of all that, a lot of the time I was depressed, unhappy and disconnected from myself and my family."

Taking a stand for your needs and making your self-renewal a priority takes courage.

Committing to this road less traveled requires you to:

Live inside out rather than outside in

Follow your heart and listen to your intuition

Care for yourself regardless of what others may think

Pause to identify and connect with your needs and desires

Say no to what drains you so you can say yes to what matters most

Continually take time to reconnect with who you are

Ask for and allow yourself to receive help

Slow down to be more present

Identify and honor your deepest values

Be gentle with yourself

Connect with your inner wisdom, your wise self

SELF-CARE = LIVING INSIDE OUT

Self-care is the foundation for becoming a courageous parent. It's not about pampering; it's about owning your personal power. It's about self-worth and honoring the person you are. And, I believe, it's your spiritual birthright.

More than ever, thousands of us are hitting the pause button and reflecting on what's really important in life. We're realizing our external environment can change on a dime. And, we're seeing how essential it is that our actions, words, thoughts, and parenting decisions align with our internal wisdom and core values.

When you allow your inner landscape to be as big as your outer landscape, your life will begin to radically, positively change. What would living from the inside out look like for you? For some this means:

Living and parenting more intentionally

Living a life that is driven by internal values, as opposed to external or societal values

Living from a place of peace rather than a place of fear (and making decisions that are reflective of this)

Responding to circumstances rather than reacting to them

I have a quote, attributed to Goethe, taped to my computer, which reminds me daily to live life inside out: "Things which matter most should never be at the mercy of things which matter least."

What reminders will you surround yourself with to help you remember to connect with and nurture your needs? Support is essential. Take time to consciously build a community of friends, colleagues, and mentors who also believe in the transformative power of self-care.

Mothers hold a powerful and pivotal role in their family's overall well-being. Having grown up with a mother who struggled with self-acceptance all her life, I know this down to my bones. When a mother feels that her needs matter and are being met, when she begins to understand that she's more than a taskmaster, and when she starts to *like* and hopefully, in time, *love* herself, the effect on her immediate family, extended family, and community is enormous.

We are all affected by one another more than we can fathom.

When women gather in a supportive, empowering environment – such as a Personal Renewal Group or other women's circle – to share insights and validate one another's experiences and needs, this can have a huge, long-reaching impact on society as a whole. As more and more women begin to make their self-care a priority, a real possibility emerges to permanently shift our culture so we are all living from the inside out, rather than the outside in.

And the self-care pebbles that each of us drop in the pond today will create ripples for generations to come.

INSPIRATION AND EXERCISES

To support you in integrating the concept of self-care into your everyday life, below you'll find three short exercises and several stories from Personal Renewal Group members on the power of self-care.

> I have always felt I needed to do my personal best all times because I have to fulfill my potential and the expectations of others. At first I thought it was "nurture" – maybe my parents' standards were too high, they did not give enough praise or I was feeling pressure as the oldest child. Then I leaned more toward "nature" – maybe I was just born with this perfectionist drive and need to please. And then one night in my Personal

Renewal Group, I had my light bulb moment. I discovered that doing many things well or at least appearing to excel feeds my ego and supports my self-confidence. Also, the high of overachieving is addictive. I think I was defining myself, and letting others perceive me, solely through my deeds. More than a few people had jokingly called me "Martha," and that was not a good thing. My work in my PRG has been life changing. It's helped me shift my perspective. I've had the opportunity to slow down enough to think about things I would never have thought of before.

$\sim$ Misty, mom to Ian, seven, and Eliot, four

EXERCISE: GUIDED JOURNALING ON MAKING YOUR SELF-CARE A PRIORITY

Set aside twenty minutes for some quiet reflection. Get comfortable: put on some cozy clothes and make some hot or iced herbal tea. Have your journal nearby in case you want to elaborate on the exercise below. If the concept of self-care is new to you, take it slowly and ease into this.

• What do *you* need (physically, emotionally, spiritually, and mentally) to be the best person, mom and partner you can be? Remember, each woman's response will be vastly different.

_____

_____

• What steps can you begin to take this month to make your self-care a priority?

_____

_____

• Which area of self-care (physical, emotional, mental, or spiritual) do you most need to focus on right now?

_____

_____

• What would motivate you to make your self-renewal a priority?

_____

_____

• Look back at the **Why Self-care?** list from earlier in the chapter and list your top three reasons for practicing self-care.

_____

_____

> As the mother of two children with special needs, I have learned the importance of putting on my oxygen mask before serving my children or anyone else. And for me, that means making time to get centered and quiet – to simply breathe and be present in the moment. It is remembering who I am and why I am here. It is also about seeing the Divine within me and others, and knowing there are gifts to discover in all that life brings us. My precious sons remind me daily to slow down, to listen to the still, small voice inside of me that is our Source, and tap into the wellspring found within all of us. I also realize that taking care of myself and my spiritual needs – whether that's going for a walk in nature, meditating, praying, practicing yoga, or being involved in a spiritual community – helps me to be a better mother and partner.
>
> ∼ Rhonda, mom to Bryan, nine, and Dylan, six

EXERCISE: GET SUPPORT
FOR YOUR SELF-CARE PRACTICE

Call and set up a dinner or coffee date with a friend or trusted mentor. Share this chapter and the exercise above with them before your date. When you meet, take turns sharing your answers to the questions above. When discussing the steps you can begin to take this month to make your self-care a priority, be specific.

I recommend you commit to consciously practicing self-care for a month. During that time, notice when and if the four areas of self-care – physical, mental, emotional, spiritual renewal – cross your radar.

Check in with your friend thirty days after your date to see how things are going (or more often if you can). And above all, be easy on yourself and don't forget: baby steps.

> I walked away from my life as a music business execu-
> tive for a more balanced existence. I created a career
> that supported that, but I found myself really resistant
> to taking time for me and my needs. After my involve-
> ment in my Personal Renewal Group, I realized that
> I had to come first, even before my daughter. I began
> to see that the life I desired was possible. It all begins
> within me and balance follows. Don't get me wrong,
> that perfectionist is still inside me, but I am so much
> more willing to look at my motivation and my deep-
> est desires before I commit to things. The greatest gift
> I have learned in the last year is that saying no brings
> abundance. The more I say no to opportunities that
> don't feed my desire for balance, the more opportuni-
> ties that support me make themselves available.
>
> ⁓ Wendy, mom to Ruby, nine

EXERCISE: TAKE FIVE MORNING CHECKUP

For the next thirty days, every morning before you step out of bed, take five minutes to mentally scan your body and check in with how you're feeling. Ask yourself, *What do I need to feel nurtured and to function at my best today?*

Remember the four areas of self-care: emotional, physical, mental, and spiritual. Make it a priority to address whatever comes up for you, even if it means saying no to something or altering your schedule for the day. Maybe you need a massage or to go for a walk. Perhaps you need to cut back on caffeine or sugar, get more sleep, start taking weekly solo dates or find a therapist or coach for support on relationship or career issues. Maybe you need to go to dinner with a friend you haven't seen in a while and reconnect. Taking a minute to do a self-care checkup sends a message to yourself that you're committed to your well-being. Your life will begin to radically change once you start to feel loved, nurtured, and truly in tune with your own needs. And your children and family will benefit immeasurably!

Tools for Career Reinvention

Kella Hatcher and Maryanne Perrin

Kella Hatcher and Maryanne Perrin are the founders of Balancing Professionals, LLC. Through their research, writing, training, and consulting, they seek to redefine work by promoting workplace flexibility as a savvy strategy that benefits employers, employees, the community, and the environment. They are also the authors of *The On-Ramping Guide: Tips, Exercises, and Important Job Search Steps for Returning to Work After Time Out Raising Kids*. You can learn more about their work and access additional resources at www.BalancingProfessionals.com.

Many of us have lamented the fact that babies don't come with an instruction manual. Yet think of all the resources out there to give us a heads up on what to expect with pregnancy, childbirth, and infancy. Despite all the great advice, solicited and unsolicited, we received to prepare for parenthood, many of us swaddled our bundles of joy and proudly brought them home not realizing we had a knowledge gap about how to integrate parenting with our careers. Unfortunately, there is no instruction manual and few conversations to give us a heads up on all the conflicts, frustrations, and fears many of us will inevitably face in determining how career and parenting fit together at different stages of our lives. Part of being a courageous parent is putting the time and effort into thinking about long-term parenting–career interconnectedness and remaining flexible to deal with immediate parenting–career dilemmas.

Parenting fears often stem from what we perceive to be a "clash" between work and family. We fear the negative impact that our work might have on our families and that our families might have on our overall careers: Am I home enough to meet my family's needs? Can I limit parenting distractions enough to be really focused on work? But we also fear the negative impact that *not* working might have on our families and careers: Can we meet our financial needs if I don't work? Will I go crazy being at home all day with kids?

Has any parent out there *not* lost sleep over such fears? The first step in easing these worries is to stop perceiving them as a "clash" between work and family, but instead as pointers that will guide your evolving strategy to integrate parenting and your career in a way that will benefit your children, yourself as a professional, and your family as a whole. The key is being intentional: Twenty years from now, when a new parent asks you to tell the story of your experience integrating parenting and work, do you want the story to be of a path that just sort of unfolded as time went on with you reacting to circumstances? Or do you want the story to be of a path that you actively created and supported with intentional thinking and actions?

In our work promoting workplace flexibility, as well as our personal experiences, we've found that parents typically fall into one of three categories when it comes to parenting-career integration. You may end up shifting categories as life brings new stages with new challenges. (We've been in each of these categories ourselves!)

On-rampers and off-rampers: Those seeking to get back into the workforce after taking time out with kids, or those seeking to leave the workforce for a time to be home with kids

Reshapers: Those seeking to make adjustments to the work arrangement of a current job in order to better balance parenting and work

Free agents and changers: Those seeking a way to be self-employed, or those seeking a new job or career, in an effort to better balance parenting and work

WORKING BACKWARDS TO DEFINE YOUR DEAL BREAKERS AND DREAM MAKERS

Ending up with the parenting-career integration that works for you requires working backwards. That is, you can't get to where you want to be if you haven't defined where you are and what you need to get there. In order to build a strategy for successful parenting-career integration, you need to start by taking stock of both your short- and long-term fears and goals. So much of fear is uncertainty, and so much of uncertainty stems from not taking the time to think through things . . . so get ready to do some thinking!

Start by picking up your pen (or keyboard) and writing down your thoughts on a blank page. There's no right or wrong, no reasonable or unreasonable: just the naked truth of what's in your head. When it comes to integrating parenting and your career, what exactly are your fears? What are your goals? A fear can be something as broad as, "I'm afraid I can never be really successful at parenting or my career as long as I try to do both," or as specific as, "I'm afraid of not being home in time to meet the school bus." A goal can be as broad as, "I want to contribute to our family's financial security," or as specific as, "we should have family dinners at least four times per week."

Once you've tapped your brain and dumped some thoughts onto paper, it's time to create a list of your needs and wants in regard to career and family. The list should have two columns: "Deal Breakers" and "Dream Makers."

Your deal breakers and dream makers utilize the results of your "brain dump" regarding fears and goals to create the backbone of your parenting–career integration strategy. Deal breakers are things that you absolutely must have in order to make work and parenting compatible and manageable – things you are not willing to sacrifice on either the family front or the career front. Dream makers are things that would support and improve parenting–career integration but that aren't absolute deal breakers – things that would move you toward your "dream" situation and are worth striving for. And remember, one person's deal breaker can be another person's dream maker and vice versa; and, as your circumstances change, items on your own dream makers and deal breakers list can swap places.

Deal Breaker Examples

- I need a job that brings in enough money to pay the mortgage

- I need a job that utilizes my [marketing, HR, financial] skills

- Since my spouse has a demanding job and can't help at home much, my income needs to be enough to pay for housecleaning (or other support services)

- I have to be in a situation that won't jeopardize my career goal [becoming CEO of the company; being a business owner; getting promoted]

- I need to be able to work from home [all the time; one day per week; as needed]

- I need a job that is challenging but not so stressful that I gain personal problems [lose sleep; can't focus on my family; struggle to take care of myself]

- I need a job that provides health insurance

- I can't work more than [twenty, thirty, forty] hours per week

- My spouse needs to be making an annual salary of [$] in order for us to afford for me to stop working and stay home

- Stepping out of the workforce will only make sense if, while I am out, I can accomplish personal career goals [get additional education or training for my next job; find some small contract work to stay connected to my profession]

- I will only start a business if I can find a good business partner

Keep in mind that anything on the deal breaker list above could be a dream maker instead.

Dream Maker Examples

- I want a job with a schedule that allows me to continue to do things that are important to me [train for triathlons, volunteer]

- I want a job with an employer who will help pay for me to get a degree

- I want a job that allows me to [work for a cause I care about; make the most of my need to be with people]

- I want my spouse to be able to help me [with cleaning; picking up the kids from day care; staying home with the kids when they're sick]

- I want to make enough money to afford a nanny instead of day care

- I want a situation where I am my own boss

Keep in mind that anything on the dream maker list above could be a deal breaker instead for some people.

Your list of deal breakers and dream makers is something you keep in your back pocket to guide you with decision making, prioritizing, and working toward goals. Your parenting–career strategy should be built first around deal breakers and second around dream makers. You should regularly reevaluate and reconfigure your list to fit your short- and long-term goals. Some items on your list may remain the same, and others will change to accommodate current circumstances or to reflect changed priorities or goals. The point of the list is not that its contents are set in stone; the point of the list is to remind you to think about parenting–career integration and be intentional about how you handle things.

CONFIDENCE AND FOCUS

If you're an on-ramper or changer, you may need to assess your confidence level and adopt the positive attitude necessary for success in a new job or career. You may also need to adjust your focus, matching your skills and interests to the type of work that's right for you.

It isn't unusual for people who have been out of the workforce or who are looking to make a change to struggle with confidence and identity. Yet problems with confidence, identity, or attitude could sabotage your quest to go back to work or make a change, so make sure your confidence and attitude are where they need to be. Also, take the time to identify your skills and interests so you can focus on the type of work that is likely to be a great match for you. Being someone who is "fine doing anything" isn't going to impress a prospective employer or land you in the right career situation – you want to be someone who is enthusiastic about doing something specific that you are really good at! There are lots of resources out there to help you with confidence or focus – consider the following:

StrengthsFinder 2.0 by Tom Rath (a book and assessment to find your strengths)

Personality and abilities assessments such as the Myers-Briggs Type Indicator, DISC, and the Highlands Ability Battery

Life or career coaches (in person or by phone)

BUILD ON WHAT YOU HAVE

Your parenting–career integration strategy stands the best chance of success if you build on what you already have rather than rushing to start from scratch. Remember that the grass is *not* always greener on the other side! If you are in a work situation that has a lot of positive attributes going for it, it is far easier to build on your track record at your current job and attempt to reshape that situation than to quit and start over looking for the "perfect" situation, which is likely quite hard to find. If you can't reshape your job but you love your field, build on your experience in that field to do contract work, start a business, or do the same work elsewhere rather than jumping to switch your field of work to accommodate your needs. If you are a solo business owner frustrated by the demands of your business, don't give up on what you've built before considering whether getting a business partner or initiating a merger with another company will address your needs. If you don't like the field of work you are in, build on the skills you like using in that field to identify a new direction to take rather than making a leap to something wildly different just because it's different. If you aren't doing paid work but are volunteering, view the skills you use in your volunteer work as a building block to support your overall experience when you seek a new job.

One of the most important things you should build on is your network. Whether you are in or out of the workforce, whether you are a reshaper, a changer, or a free agent, you *need* a network and you need to be intentional about building and maintaining it. Believe it or not, networking is not a dirty concept like spamming or telemarketing or pyramid scheming. The substance of networking is not about small talk, trading business cards, or trying to get someone to do something for you for free. Networking is about relationships; it is about finding ways to help others as much or more than they help you. Networking is key to parenting–career integration at any stage because, let's face it, our relationships with people can pretty much make or break anything we do in life, including our ability to integrate parenting and careers.

Networking starts by building on the relationships and skills you already have to form new relationships and acquire or strengthen skills. All of us have existing networks. There are networks of co-workers, networks of colleagues in your field, networks of soccer parents, networks of PTA volunteers, networks of neighbors – the list goes on and on. People in a network can keep each other sane with morning walks, help connect each other to work opportunities, trade emergency child care help, learn each others' strengths by working side by side on a volunteer project, and support or mentor each other in the workplace. Building and maintaining your network may involve joining an organization that is focused on your skills or interests, or it might mean striking up a conversation on the soccer sidelines to get to know another parent a little better. For on-rampers, a common challenge is reconnecting with your professional identity and putting this "self" forward in networking situations. What's important is to be intentional about building and maintaining your network of relationships to help you navigate your current situation and help take you to the next step on your parenting–career path.

BE EDUCATED

Many modern parents will find themselves seeking some type of nontraditional work arrangement or nontraditional career path at some point in order to better integrate parenting and work. It is important to know that the traditional one-size-fits-all workplace structure, characterized by the full-time, on-site job, is taking some of its last breaths. When you look at things in this context it can be empowering to know that you are one among many, many people who desire alternative ways to work. Why will the typical one-size-fits-all approach to work need to change in the coming years?

We work and live in a global economy. Work simply looks different when you are connecting with customers and colleagues in different time zones and locations. It's silly to think we can take the Industrial Age workplace model (employees working on the same schedule from the same location) and expect it to serve us well in an information-based workplace. It doesn't!

The structure of our society has changed significantly. Sixty years ago, two-thirds of American households had an adult home during the day to deal with the demands of everyday life. Today, due to the rise in both dual-earner and single-parent households, that number has dropped to less than one in four. Work and life are colliding more than ever before and workers are seeking new ways of working so they can effectively manage both.

Major demographic groups are calling for alternative ways to work. Working moms have been the torch-bearers for alternative work arrangements for years: a 2007 Pew Research Center study showed that sixty percent of working mothers viewed "part-time" as the ideal work arrangement. The good news is, other demographic groups have added their voice to the cause, making it hard to ignore. A 2009 study by the Center for Work-Life Policy showed that workplace flexibility is important to 89 percent of Generation Ys and 87 percent of Baby Boomers.

Technology has redefined how we do everything. When you can work from the soccer sidelines in the afternoon or your kitchen table at midnight or shop from your desk at work, the boundaries between work and life have clearly blurred. Need we say more?

ALTERNATIVES TO THE LADDER

Once upon a time, many of us dreamed of climbing a career ladder. Then some of us got on the ladder and realized that the rungs, up or down, didn't offer a lot of options – only traditional, in-the-office, morning-to-evening, Monday-through-Friday work situations – and that these options often didn't mesh with the realities of our lives. Others got on the ladder only to watch it deteriorate as offshoring, out-of-control health care costs, and a whopper of a recession ended the notion of a long-term career at a single employer. What are some of the alternatives to the traditional career ladder?

Part-time work. As we pointed out earlier, finding a smaller "plate" of work is attractive for many parents because it is a great way to balance the demands of work and family. Job sharing, where two professionals share one job in a 50/50 or other split, is an under-utilized part-time strategy that provides employers with full-time coverage and other advantages, such as being able to call in two people during intensive all-hands-on-deck events.

Telecommuting. Working all or a portion of your job from home can be great for your productivity and save you the time, money, and stress involved in commuting. For example, Cisco's 2009 study of the impact of its telecommuting policies found an estimated annual productivity savings of $277 million! The ability to work from home now and then may be all you need to manage the balancing act between the work front and the home front.

Contract work. As the world of lifetime-employment changes, many companies are turning to contract employees – freelancers – as a solution to project-based work. If you have a skill that is conducive to project-based work – such as writing, editing, programming, web development, graphic design, or consulting – you are good at networking, you are comfortable with a less predictable financial source, and you are willing to forego employer-sponsored benefits like health insurance and retirement, freelancing may be a great option for you.

Entrepreneurship and partnership. According to the Center for Women's Business Research, in 2008–2009 there were over 7.2 million majority-women-owned firms in the United States. This explosion in the growth of women-owned businesses is a sign that women are taking charge and creating the professional autonomy and flexibility they need. The Internet has also lowered many hurdles making entrepreneurship a more low-cost, low-risk alternative than ever before. Have a great idea burning in your belly? Consider becoming your own boss and making it happen.

There *are* innovative employers who have dismantled the career ladder as we know it and are instead offering employees greater control of their career paths and work situations. One example is Deloitte, the public accounting firm with a significant female employee base, who has always been a leader in workplace flexibility. They estimate that in 2003 alone workplace flexibility saved them $27 million in avoided turnover costs. Realizing that a corporate *ladder* didn't offer a viable strategy for many talented employees who sought a nonlinear path – by slowing down or stepping out at times to deal with children, elders, and other life events – Deloitte developed a *lattice* framework called Mass Career Customization. Employees now have a framework allowing them to dial-up or dial-down on four key elements: pace, workload, location/schedule, and role. You can learn more about MCC by reading *Mass Career Customization: Aligning the Workplace with Today's Nontraditional Workforce* by Cathy Benko. Best Buy is another innovator in workplace flexibility. Their Results-Only Work Environment (ROWE) system allows corporate employees to work when and where they want as long as they get the job done. ROWE has resulted in a forty percent increase in productivity, increased customer satisfaction, decreased turnover, and various other benefits to the company. You can learn more about ROWE by visiting www.culturerx.com.

BE CREATIVE AND PERSISTENT

If only our perfect jobs were readily available by scanning the newspaper, or better yet, having them offered up to us by an astute manager who is tuned in to our individual work–life needs. The reality is that you are going to have to think outside the box and use a variety of strategies to create your next good career opportunity. (We know it likely won't be perfect, that's why you have your list of deal breakers.) What follows are a few examples of using creativity and persistence to get where you want to be.

On-rampers or changers seeking an arrangement other than the traditional full-time job might be discouraged by the dearth of advertised positions. Our advice: if you see a full-time job that is a great fit for you, apply anyway! Your schedule or options to telecommute are both things that can be negotiated, just like salary and vacation time. An alternative schedule is probably not the first thing you want to bring up in an interview, but once you and the company have learned about each other and established mutual interest, then you can begin to explore the options. More advice for navigating the complete on-ramping process can be found in our new guide, *The On-Ramping Guide: Tips, Exercises, and Important Job Search Steps for Returning to Work After Time Out Raising Kids*, available from our Web site.

As we talk with professionals, we are often surprised at how many folks leave an existing job *before* they think creatively about potential changes – reduced hours, some telecommuting, job sharing, a different schedule – and ask for them. Don't jump to being a changer or free agent before you consider being a reshaper! Asking never hurts and you might be surprised to find that you get what you want, especially if you've done your homework (more on that in a minute).

We can recommend the reshaper strategy from personal experience: Kella loved a lot of things about her legal counsel job except the workload, so she proposed turning her position into a job-share arrangement. Although job sharing had never been done at her organization, her boss agreed. We think job sharing is a powerful strategy with a great deal of growth potential. As a tech company executive, Maryanne was struggling with child care dilemmas before her first child was born, as were some colleagues who were having babies around the same time. When they approached their bosses about the situation, the managers were willing to set up an onsite nursery – a win-win for everyone.

Finally, the creative strategy of volunteering your time and expertise can serve you well whether you are an on-ramper, changer, or free agent. It might not be the quickest route to a new job or new client, but it is a great way to get important experience and build a network that can refer you to other opportunities. Be smart in the volunteer opportunities you target – choose ones that give you exposure to an industry, cause, or profession that interests you and is likely to lead to worthwhile connections.

BE TECH SAVVY

Without technology, many of our favorite ways to integrate parenting and careers (working a variety of schedules from a variety of locations) would not be possible. Technology is also a powerful enabler when it comes to building and maintaining your network, so our advice is to embrace technology and think of it as your friend. Below are just a few examples of how you can leverage technology.

Participate in social networking Web sites. Social networking (connecting with people online) is a growing trend and can be a great complement to some of the more traditional avenues for networking in your job search. While the list of networking services really is endless (new services are born every day) consider using LinkedIn for professional networking, to connect with former colleagues and classmates, search for job openings, and find warm leads into companies you are targeting. Facebook is another popular tool used primarily for building your personal network. Our caveat with Facebook: make sure to modify your privacy settings so that potential employers or clients won't have access to your personal Facebook page. Regardless of your privacy settings, it is a good idea to avoid posting anything you'd be uncomfortable with a client or employer seeing as privacy settings are complex and Facebook changes them from time to time.

Stay connected and perform your job even when you aren't in the office. If your boss and your co-workers see that you can respond to job demands when you aren't in the office, it will go a long way to them accepting your work arrangement. Consider having a smart phone and remote access to your work computer from your home computer – both will allow you to handle email communication when you aren't in the office.

Use technology to support a job-share arrangement. Many job sharers we know share a voicemail box and an email address, which allows them to operate as "one front" to their customers.

Embrace other tools that allow you to work anywhere, anytime. The more comfortable you are using collaboration tools such as virtual meeting applications, screen sharing technologies, and document management tools, the more you'll be able to control when and where you work.

BE PREPARED

What is your best defense against the resistance you might meet from others as you navigate career transitions? *Anticipating* and *addressing*. By anticipating issues and concerns and then proactively addressing them, you are likely to prevent molehills from turning into mountains. Ready to get prepared?

Do your homework. Anticipate the impact of your career change on yourself, your family, your boss, and your co-workers. What are the likely challenges each may face? Are there skills that you need to beef up to land your desired job? Do you need to restock your professional wardrobe? Will your family need additional child care or a revision in household responsibilities based on changing finances or changing schedules? What concerns might your boss have if you are proposing an alternative work arrangement? What about your co-workers?

Map out a plan. Now that you've anticipated where you or others might get stuck, it's time to map out a written plan for the situation you desire. Be sure to address any anticipated concerns an employer might have, such as availability, responsiveness, access to you if you are not physically present, and who provides for office and equipment use. Likewise, you'll want to address potential concerns that your spouse might have, such as who handles child care pickup and specific household chores. Having thought through and documented things can help ease a spouse or future employer's doubts and make them willing to give it a trial run.

Show that it's a win-win. With an employer, it's critical to focus on the win-win of the proposed arrangement and not on the reason you are seeking it. Are there financial savings to the employer, such as low or no benefit costs, prorated salaries, and saved office space? Show them in the proposal. If you are proposing a job share, point out that there is backup coverage built into the position and two minds for the price of one! Show that you are willing to be flexible, too, by taking calls from home on non-work days or rearranging your schedule to attend important meetings. This can go a long way in overcoming resistance.

ASSESS, TWEAK, AND BE OPEN TO CHANGE!

No matter how much planning you do, things inevitably will change. Your deal breakers and dream makers may be different at various stages in your life; these changes may be self-imposed or they may be dictated by influences you can't control, such as the economy, access to health insurance, or the failing health of an aging parent. If you can think about your career path as a lattice instead of a ladder – one that can take you to many interesting destinations versus one ultimate destination – you'll appreciate the opportunity to assess and tweak as a means for better integrating work and family. After all, it really is about the journey and not just the destination!

section two

Developing Your Own Courageous Parenting Style

Developing our own courageous parenting style stems from trusting our instincts and giving our children freedom within limits. In "The Courage to Let Our Kids Solve Their Own Problems," Maya Frost shares her family's story, which involved weaving together international travel and education in ways that gave each of her four daughters plenty of opportunities to grow into independent young women. Her daughter Talya's experience attending high school in Mexico, at a time when Maya and her husband Tom spoke little Spanish, was a challenging and rewarding adventure for all of them. Maya discusses the difference between giving needed guidance to teens and jumping in to rescue them out of our own fear and ego – an insidious combination that she has dubbed "fego."

Next, Melissa Stanton cuts through the mystique of parenting experts to talk about ways that each of us can develop our own expertise, leavened with a sense of humor, humility, and the understanding that there is no one perfect way to parent. Melissa's years of experience working in magazine publishing gave her a behind-the-scenes look at parenting experts that allows her to debunk their all-knowing aura. Her life as a stay-at-home mother of three, including twins, has shown her the value of real-world parenting experience, and has illuminated the fact that while life is never easy, most of us are doing the best we can. In her chapter, she encourages each of us to develop "The Courage to Become Your Own Parenting 'Expert.'"

While there are many ways to be a good parent, I strongly believe that Positive Discipline is a style worth studying and implementing. Parent educator Amy McCready, founder of Positive Parenting Solutions, introduces this parenting strategy, which is noted for being both effective and respectful to all family members. While there are many aspects to Positive Discipline, Amy emphasizes "The Power of Personal Significance for Kids of All Ages."

Incessant worrying can keep us from giving our kids the experiences they need to become independent adults. Leadership consultant and author of *Mom-in-Chief* Jamie Woolf explores the
advantages and challenges of three different parenting "modes."
Whether each of us is a Liberator, Connector, or Achiever, we can
leverage our natural strengths and feel more joy and success in
what we do once we're aware of our individual preferred leadership style. One mode is not better than another: the key is to stay
true to yourself. In "I'm Worried I Worry Too Much, But How
Do I Stop?" Jamie helps parents learn how to work with their own
style in a way that decreases unnecessary worry and anxiety.

The Courage to Let Our Kids Solve Their Own Problems

Maya Frost

Maya Frost is an American writer, mindfulness trainer, and international lifestyle design consultant living in Argentina and Uruguay. She is the mother of four recently launched daughters and the author of *The New Global Student: Skip the SAT, Save Thousands on Tuition, and Get a Truly International Education.* Learn more at www.MayaFrost.com.

One of the hardest things for any parent of teenagers to face is learning how to step back and allow our kids to struggle rather than step in and solve all their problems for them. What might help them in the short-term ends up hurting them in the long-term: by protecting them from the bumps and bruises of life, we are blocking their path to becoming confident and competent young adults.

Bold parenting requires doing some serious work on *ourselves* in order to let our children grow up. When I think about what it means to be a bold parent, I don't picture fighting for school funding or a new sports field or more books. While those are strong actions in support of kids in general, they are not battles about parenting *per se*. And I don't think it's particularly brave or noble for parents to sacrifice everything to send their kids to the most elite schools. In many instances, this is much more a case of parents being driven by ego rather than their kids' best interests. Ultimately, pushing our high school-aged sons and daughters forward in the direction *we* feel is best for them is often a fear-based action that many parents confuse with mentoring.

As mentors, however, our role is to encourage and support our teenagers, make sure they understand the range of options available to them, and then (deep breath) *allow them to make their own choices*. Parenting is a continuous process of loving, nurturing, and letting go – even when it hurts. Our job is to ensure that our sons and daughters become strong and independent young adults who care about others, know their own gifts, and share them with the world in whatever way they choose.

No parent sets out to zealously overprotect their kids, but it's hard to separate everyday concerns into piles clearly marked "step in" and "let go." So we look around at what other parents are doing, and when in doubt, tend to overstep because that's how other fear-affected parents are behaving. In addition, we worry about being judged as too casual or too lenient – the slacker parent who is failing to take charge. This one-two punch of fear and ego – a sneaky combo I call "fego" – gets in the way of making the choices that are truly best for our kids. As parents, we must learn to check our natural tendency to hover while still retaining a reasonable amount of concern for the safety and success of our children. It's a fine balance, and one that gets harder to maintain in the face of media and peer pressure.

The first step in overcoming fego and becoming a supportive mentor (rather than a fearful protector or over-involved coach) is to become aware of how our own emotions direct us. In any given challenge – an argument, a school or relationship issue, a struggle over changing rules and roles as our kids get older – we naturally deal with what it brings up in us *first* before turning to how it affects our child. And once we get caught in that web of fear (about how the situation might affect our child) and ego (about protecting our view of ourselves as good parents), we tend to stay there, rather than shifting the focus to our teenager.

This is the root of most parent-child conflict in the teen years: what seems to be right from *our* perspective is not necessarily what the child needs or wants. We must find a way to communicate and reach a consensus rather than turning each challenge into a battle with a winner and a loser. The key for parents is to pause long enough to see this clearly rather than getting wrapped up in the struggle for control.

Developing the ability to refocus our attention on our kids rather than ourselves takes practice, and the sooner you start, the easier it will be. From my consulting experience helping parents raise competent, confident, and compassionate kids, I've seen that those who get good at letting go in baby steps are the ones who proudly watch their kids head off on adventures of their own as teenagers while maintaining close and loving relationships with them. My husband and I had had plenty of opportunities to practice this stepping back with our own four daughters – and then we upped the ante by moving abroad when they were teenagers.

OUR ADVENTURE ABROAD

In 2005, my husband and I decided to sell everything and leave our suburban American lifestyle behind for a family adventure abroad. We felt strongly that our kids would benefit tremendously from spending time developing a broader perspective of the world – not to mention an unbeatable skill set for life in the global economy – and we saw that we had a small window of opportunity to experience life abroad as a family before our girls all scattered for college. We'd already encouraged the three oldest to spend their junior year of high school abroad on a Rotary Youth Exchange year, just as my husband and his three siblings had twenty years earlier. We'd watched our two oldest teens return from their exchanges with greater self-assurance, endless stories of amazing experiences, and a passion for connecting with those in other countries. We knew that spending a substantial period of time abroad as a family would exponentially expand their awareness of the world and their own possibilities.

Most parents wouldn't take on the challenge of moving abroad with teenagers, but we'd already seen that our kids (the oldest two, anyway) were capable of thriving during a year abroad *without* us, so it didn't seem like much of a leap to move abroad as a family! After all, we'd have each other to lean on, and the move would bind us even more closely together and give us a lifetime of shared stories. Plus, we knew from our previous trips (including a three-month sabbatical to India and Nepal when they were 7, 8, 10 and 11) that our most exhilarating and rewarding moments were those we'd shared in places that challenged us as individuals and as a family unit. Still, we never expected it to be easy. It's hard enough raising four teenage daughters, but we had the added challenge of guiding them through the process of discovering who they were without their friends, activities, and identities "back home" while ushering them through high school and into college in nontraditional ways.

When we moved to Mexico, our daughters were 14, 15, 17, and 18. The 15-year-old had just left for a year-long exchange in Brazil, and the 18-year-old was already in college, so we started our journey with just the 14-year-old and the 17-year-old, who had just returned from her year-long exchange (in Brazil as well, as it turned out). I can see now that we viewed it as simply the biggest in a series of transitions for our family – there was always a daughter preparing to go abroad, getting ready to return home, or getting used to being back!

Parents of high school exchange students have to become masters at letting go. Believe me, there have been many times when I struggled as I watched them go through the process of leaving, being homesick, fumbling their way through the experience of living with a new family, making new friends, and understanding new rules about life in an unfamiliar place. And I have shed my own tears (mostly surreptitiously) while listening to them shed theirs. Consequently, we felt primed for the challenge of making this big family move based on our past successes, but our greatest confidence came from the fact that we really knew our kids – their strengths, their worries, their idiosyncrasies, and their capacity for growth. In addition, we trusted that we as parents could roll with the punches and ensure that each of our daughters – including the ones who were not moving with us – would get the support and encouragement they needed from us in order to thrive.

Knowing the importance of including our kids in family decisions, we had many heart-to-heart talks with our girls about the move, never glossing over the fact that it would be very difficult at times. We were especially focused on making sure that our youngest daughter, Talya, understood what she was giving up: she would not have a single year of high school in the United States. We did our best to make sure she understood what challenges she was taking on, and she insisted that she was up for it.

Of course, there was no way for us to know what was *really* ahead. And Talya herself has expressed many times since then that she was glad she was so naïve. Had she known how hard it would be, she might have asked us not to move and missed out on the most incredibly transformational year of her life.

So with Talya's wholehearted enthusiasm, we enrolled her in

her first year of high school – as the only foreigner in a Spanish-speaking high school in Mazatlan. As Talya was our fourth teenager, we felt prepared simply because we already knew that there are plenty of tearful days in high school *anywhere*. Though our girls had been happy in high school, even the stuff of high school girls' dreams – the games, the dates, the proms, the parties – can resemble nightmares more often than Disney movies. I'd watched my older girls go through their frustrations with gossip, idiotic boyfriends, misunderstandings with close friends, and most markedly, reintegrating into high school after being abroad for a year. I knew that what Talya would experience in Mexico would be far more meaningful and ultimately much more positive than the petty squabbles and dull disappointments that often characterized high school back home.

And we had a surprising head start in terms of letting go: my husband and I could not step in to solve all of Talya's problems because we did not speak Spanish well. This forced Talya to become responsible for much of her own experience in Mexico. Looking back on it, we all see this as a huge blessing: there was no way for us to overstep our roles because we were incapable of doing so! Our natural parental tendency to step in was curtailed by our language limitations *just enough* to make us have to think about what we were doing before interfering. Most of the time, parents don't have that barrier – nothing slows us down, so we don't have the ability to see what might happen if we don't try to save the day. In my work as a mindfulness trainer, I see again and again how taking *just a brief moment* to pause before acting can make the difference between responding impulsively and proceeding with awareness and intention. The language barrier worked in our favor because we were always just a beat behind – and this was just enough time for Talya to respond in her own way.

Though there were certainly moments when we felt inadequate

as parents, we were experienced enough to know that this isn't terribly unusual – *most* parents feel inadequate at times! We'd had plenty of opportunities to experience doubt about our parenting with our three older daughters, so perhaps we just weren't afraid of it. In fact, I think that putting ourselves in a position of being incapable of being perfect parents was a brilliant decision on our part – it helped our daughters see us as people and understand that when they became adults they weren't required to be perfect, either. Being a doofus on occasion can be quite liberating – not to mention hilarious! Mexico gave us an opportunity to lighten up and let go of the notion that we had to be in control of things. Life doesn't always go as planned, but teaching your kids how to handle the unexpected is so much more important than protecting them from it.

Still, it was hard to watch Talya go through the struggles of daily life. Her experience was like American high school on steroids – in Mexico, in Spanish, and as a very conspicuous new kid. It didn't help that she'd always been a sensitive child. She was quiet and always looked for a way to distinguish herself through overachieving. She had such a perfectionist streak that we felt it would be beneficial for her to learn to fail and be okay with it. However, that didn't mean we wanted her to be miserable! We knew it would be tough for her to go through a year of not being the best student or beloved by all the teachers. But we also knew that she had an inner strength she had not yet tapped, and that she would thrive once she overcame her own obstacles.

We knew *she* could handle it – but could *we*?

It's especially hard for parents of emotionally sensitive kids to step back and risk their kids getting hurt. It's agonizing to acknowledge that your sweet child could be mistreated in any way, but the reality is that high school is a harsh place, particularly for those who wear their hearts on their sleeves. Talya was never one to call attention to herself – she was happiest to be in the background, quietly doing her thing. When my husband Tom and I walked her to her first day of high school in Mexico, I had so many butterflies in my stomach that I considered having my husband take her alone. But imagine what it must have been like for my daughter! She walked into the school courtyard and hundreds of heads turned toward her – as the only blonde, blue-eyed student in the entire school, her arrival was a big event. The boys called out to her (fortunately none of us could understand what they were saying), and the girls huddled in circles to talk about her. It was excruciating – at least, for Tom and me. Talya, however, looked as calm and confident as anyone who'd been going to school there forever. She's always been good at hiding her feelings, but I knew she was quaking inside.

We met her outside the school when the day was finished, and her new friends were gathered around her. She was smiling and nodding, but it was clear she couldn't understand what they were saying to her. She waved her goodbyes, and once she turned to us, her eyes filled with tears. We put our arms around her and walked the few blocks home. She told us about how exhausting the day had been: every second brought a new challenge, and she'd felt sick all day long. She wanted nothing more than to go home and go to sleep despite the fact that it was only one in the afternoon.

There were many days like that. Days when immature boys, wanting to get her attention, would steal the homework she'd slaved over and tear it to pieces. Days when girls would ignore her during break in the courtyard. Days when the teachers seemed annoyed to have her in the classroom. On those days, we felt so protective of her and upset that she had to suffer these indignities. She didn't deserve it, and as parents who had brought her there, we felt responsible. We were filled with fego: Were we causing harm? Were we terrible parents?

Ultimately, what helped most was taking our fego-based concerns out of the equation and focusing on our daughter instead. Was she feeling that she was *capable* of dealing with this, even if it was difficult? Did she need our compassion – or our help? That last question is key: too often, parents step in and fix the problem when what our kids really need is support and encouragement. My husband hates to see his daughters cry. So, like many fathers, he tends to jump in and offer logic in moments of emotion. To combat this, our mantra has become, "Hugs first, then help, if requested." This reminds us to slow down and focus on what our kids need from us rather than on what we are tempted to provide in order to make ourselves feel more comfortable!

Anyway, we did a pretty good job of being calm and supportive. Her older sister Tara, on the other hand, just got mad. She wanted to charge up to the school and smack those kids who were causing her little sister so much pain. She was ready to, as she put it, "kick some serious ass." We understood her sentiments completely, but fortunately, we talked her into staying home and comforting Talya instead. We didn't feel that the other kids were malicious in any way – they were just kids who had no clue how difficult things were for Talya and no skills to help her feel at home.

We pointed out to Talya that she could quit and be home-schooled if she liked, but she wanted to keep at it. Why? Well, in between these bad days were ones on which Talya had something happy to report – a moment when she had understood the teacher or had done something right and her classmates had applauded her. These little victories carried her forward. She spent a lot of time on her homework and looked up many words each night in order to improve her Spanish. She began to have plans with her friends instead of coming home for the midday meal after school, and she started to get invitations to parties and to the beach on the weekends. She attended several *quinceañeras*,

the extravagant Latin American 15th birthday coming-of-age cel-
ebrations, and even spent a week living at a friend's house in order
to practice her Spanish.

Each month, parents were expected to go to the school to get
their child's report card and listen to the teachers talk about what
was happening in class. Since my husband and I only knew very
basic Spanish, this proved to be an evening of embarrassment for
us, as we had to respond to the teachers' questions in front of
the group. Although the school was on a cliff with a spectacular
view of the Pacific Ocean, the classroom itself was windowless and
dingy. We marveled at how Talya could spend her days there struggling with the language and feeling constantly clueless.

As parents, we'd had no expectations for Talya in terms of academics that year. We figured it was enough just to show up and
try to absorb as much of the language and culture as possible. We
knew that the skills she was developing – and the understanding of
her own strength and abilities – were much more important than
keeping up with a certain level of math or English.

But Talya's response to feeling stupid in class was to work harder.
After about three months, she was getting top grades in all of her
classes – in fact, she was doing better than most of her classmates! She
was asked to be the chemistry tutor – in Spanish. This did amazing
things for her confidence and helped her establish herself as a good
student – though it was somewhat of a blow to realize that being a
good student didn't count for much there. Most of her friends asked
why she bothered to study so hard – what was the point?

There were many highs and lows that year, but things really got
challenging when her classmates voted for her to represent them
in the school's Spring Festival. It was her understanding that it was
an English festival of some kind and that she would have to give
a speech in English in front of all the students and parents. Since
she was the only native speaker of English in the entire school, this
seemed to make sense, and she wasn't too concerned about it.

The festival turned out to be a highly anticipated pageant that all the local girls dream about throughout their childhood years! Talya was vying for the coveted position of Spring Queen. Not only was there no English involved whatsoever, but there were many, many events required for which she was completely unprepared. She had to coordinate numerous community service events, including painting over graffiti, collecting cans, going to an orphanage, and picking up trash on the beach. She needed to figure out what to do, say, and wear during a full schedule of events, from press conferences conducted in Spanish to a formal coronation ceremony.

It turned out to be a month of both exhilaration and humiliation for her. She'd show up at an event with the wrong outfit, the wrong speech, or to find out that she was in charge of something that nobody had ever bothered to mention to her. Because she was the princess for the youngest class, most of her classmates had no knowledge of the details of the festival and were no help whatsoever. Though they'd certainly attended the parade as younger kids, they hadn't paid attention to things like what the princesses wore or how the cars were decorated. They hadn't known about "poster day" or "can drive day" so were clueless when it came to explaining these to Talya, who was in charge of coordinating these events for her class. Fortunately, toward the end, the senior class princess (who was eventually crowned queen) took pity on her and helped her out, and Talya was delighted when the most popular senior boy asked to be her escort during the formal coronation.

There were many times that month when we told her she could just quit, that it wasn't worth it, and nobody would think any less of her. But she wouldn't hear of it. She had discovered something about herself: she liked the experience of overcoming her fear. As parents, it was our job to be tuned in to her needs and be ready to help if she was getting in over her head, but it was clear that she was committed to seeing it through and didn't need or want us to make things easier for her. Obviously, not all kids would respond to this situation in the same way. In fact, I'm certain that each of our four daughters would have made different choices if they were faced with the same situation. That's why it's so important for parents to know their kids well and to recognize that there is no one-size-fits-all approach, even among siblings! Another daughter might have chosen to participate in a different way (perhaps doing the minimum required or seeking more help from classmates) or opted-out completely, but we had seen that Talya truly relished the challenge. The smartest thing we did was *ask her what she wanted to do* rather than assume she wanted to quit. We listened, and then gave her the chance to do things her way. She even went above and beyond the call of duty by writing a speech in Spanish and presenting it to the entire school! But again, that's just her. We needed to honor her wishes and allow her to have this experience in her own way, even if we had to suffer through our fego!

And suffer we did. The most fego-filled moment for me as a parent was the parade. Talya was told that she needed to organize a contingent of cars containing a few classmates and their parents that would follow her along the coast road. They told her to wear something "fun" and that she needed to provide T-shirts to her supporters so that they would be more visible.

On the morning of the parade, she was nervous but very pleased with herself. We had gone to a party supply store and ordered some balloons in her spring colors, arranged for an expat friend with a baby-blue restored fifties convertible to drive her, and purchased plain yellow T-shirts for her fans to wear and markers for them to decorate them themselves. She was excited to wear her favorite dress, a pink satin "cupcake" dress she'd worn as a bridesmaid at a casual wedding back in Oregon. It was knee-length and strapless, with a fitted bodice, a black satin sash, and a full skirt thanks to layers of netting underneath. Going with the "fun" theme, she'd added a plastic tiara and a pink feather boa.

As we entered the parade staging area, it became immediately clear that she was treating this parade very differently than the other candidates. The other princesses were dressed head to toe in tight black nightclub outfits: low-cut, with rhinestones, sequins, big hoop earrings, and stilettos. They were riding on the cabs of huge four-by-four trucks followed by at least twenty other vehicles packed with friends and family members wearing T-shirts printed with a glamour shot of their favorite princess.

There were whispers. People were pointing. I felt utterly helpless and humiliated, worried about how she must be feeling about being so obviously out of the loop. She had only five cars behind her convertible; she didn't have dozens of family members and neighbors supporting her, just a few classmates who'd shown up.

My maternal instinct was to whisk her far away from it all, to protect her and never allow her to become a spectacle like this again. I felt that I had let her down by not knowing how to help her do the "right" thing.

But while I was wallowing in my maternal angst, I turned to look at her. She was standing with a bunch of photographers who were ignoring the others and focusing on her. And she was *beaming*. She was posing for each photographer, smiling and answering questions, and she was so radiant that my heart just burst. Sure, she knew all too well that things hadn't quite gone as planned, but she'd been experiencing that every day for *months* so she'd learned to handle it. I was in awe as I watched her wave to the spectators along the parade route, smiling with joy and brandishing her tiara and feather boa with pride.

What would have happened if I had tried to protect her from potential embarrassment? What if I had allowed my concern for her (fear) and my own humiliation (ego) to dim her joy on this occasion? What would she have missed if I had stepped in?

A few nights later, watching her curtsy during the coronation in her heavenly blue gown was one of the proudest parenting moments of my life. It wasn't about winning – she came in third – it was the fact that she had made the most of a very challenging situation and fully embraced her opportunity. Anyone looking at her smiling in her beautiful dress with her handsome escort would assume that this whole festival had been a magical and glamorous affair filled with friendship and fun, the epitome of every school-girl's dream. But we knew what an ordeal it had been and how she'd had to rise to the occasion on a daily basis. And though she'd publicly smiled through nearly all of it, we'd witnessed the tears and frustration and knew that this moment capped a tumultuous year of her life that had taught her so much about herself.

In my book, *The New Global Student*, Talya shares this story and explains that her experience in Mexico gave her a tremendous amount of strength. She knows that she can literally go anywhere and do anything and that she can begin as an outsider and eventually feel at home. Now a recent college grad – she earned her BS two weeks after turning 19 – she has had some time to see how that year affected her.

> Whenever I look back on my year in Mexico, I am absolutely astounded by all that I went through and all that I accomplished. And I am so proud of myself for being strong, for loosening up, and for being open to entirely new experiences. There were countless times when I could have shut down or just refused to participate in anything. But I kept going for no other reason than I wanted to see if I could. Now, whenever I have to face a particularly challenging experience, I always

smile and remember Mexico – if I could do that, I can do anything! It made me understand how strong I really am, how much I can offer when I'm okay being who I am, and how much I can gain by allowing myself to be imperfect. It was a year that taught me how to trust myself – and how to be bold. I can't imagine who I would be now without that incredible experience.

We'd never planned to stay in Mexico longer than a year – it was for us what many expats call their "starter country," the one in which you figure out where you really want to live. And so, toward the end of that year, we asked Talya to pick the next destination. After all, she had the most schooling ahead of her, and she'd done an amazing job of making the most of the year. We knew it was possible she would say she wanted to go back to Oregon – we wouldn't have blamed her if she did, and it was a prospect we would have considered, but one that none of the rest of us would have chosen ourselves.

To her credit, she said she wanted to go to another Spanish-speaking country to improve her language skills, but she wanted a bigger city, with more diversity and opportunities for cultural learning. She did her research and picked Buenos Aires, Argentina, explaining that it was a cosmopolitan city of nearly 13 million people that offered a wide range of activities – and schools. Our oldest daughter had been there for a few days as part of her high school exchange in Chile, but other than that, none of us had ever been to Argentina and had no idea what to expect. But Talya had been thorough in her research and we'd all discussed the pros and cons. We packed our two bags each and headed to "the Paris of South America" on the fourth of July – the middle of winter.

During that first week in Buenos Aires, we accompanied Talya to her interviews at several high schools. She picked a small international school where classes were taught in both English and Spanish. The kids seemed really friendly and welcoming, and she thought it would be a good fit.

But it soon became clear to Talya that it wasn't a good fit for two reasons. First, the kids had all been together since kindergarten – and none of them were international, other than the fact that they'd learned English. They were all Argentine students; she was the only foreigner yet again, and one trying to break into a very tight group of 28 students. Second, she was completely shocked by the way the students yelled and argued about everything throughout the day. Girls screamed and boys shouted, saying terrible things that made Talya cringe. She told us that any one of these arguments would have been school-wide gossip and absolute friendship-enders back in the United States. But remarkably, the Argentine kids took none of it personally. After a typical morning of heated arguments and name-calling, the students would all go out to lunch together, chatting and laughing as though nothing had happened.

While this style of communication is very much part of Argentine culture, it completely eviscerated Talya and made it difficult for her to concentrate on studying. In addition, it turned out that because she had switched hemispheres, this semester in Buenos Aires was a repeat of her previous one in Mexico – it wouldn't count. So, we encouraged her to look at some other educational possibilities for the next few months. We told her that this experience was not meant to be about suffering – it was supposed to be about *learning*. She could always choose to start again in April once the new school year began, but in the meantime, she had a chance to learn in whatever ways she enjoyed most. It was our job to make sure she understood that she had *options*.

Ultimately, she decided to try learning in a different setting. This turned out to be an absolutely pivotal decision for her.

Even though she was only 16, she was able to sign up for intensive Spanish classes at a local university where she sat alongside college students from the United States and other countries who were there on study abroad programs. Her Spanish skills were higher than most – she was put in an intermediate-level class and was one of the top students. This boosted her confidence and proved to her that she could handle herself in a classroom with older students.

Talya also found several tutors to help her with specific topics. We encouraged her to interview each one in a safe, public place and choose the ones she thought would be best for her. We were not a part of these interviews at all – we wanted her to trust her instincts. She selected a young American attorney who was passionate about literature to guide her through the classics. Her tutor for history was a young Canadian who had taught at a university in Toronto. And she met with a young Argentine Ph.D. candidate for lessons in biology.

By spring, Talya was one of only four students in the advanced Spanish class at the university along with an MIT grad student and two bicultural students reigniting their childhood fluency. She loved the challenge of the university classroom, and we started exploring options for her to skip the rest of high school and dive right into college.

We researched a number of ways to do it, and one path emerged that would be the most affordable and immediate ticket to entry into a university as a full-time student: the GED.

Fego alert! I felt the fear and ego as we considered this option. Would she be excluded from opportunities in the future? Would we be judged as parents who were sabotaging her education?

Fortunately, we'd watched our three other daughters finish high school in alternative ways – one did a dual enrollment program, one graduated early, one finished online – and because they'd all done well in college, earning their Bachelor's degrees by 19 or 20, we were open to considering this option for Talya.

Talya decided to pursue her GED, but the organization that administered the GED tests locally in Buenos Aires required test-takers to be at least 17 years old. Because she wanted to enroll in college classes in Buenos Aires in the fall – two months before her 17th birthday – we realized that the best solution was for her to spend the summer in the United States so that she could take her test in Oregon, which had a minimum testing age of 16. So, while we stayed in Argentina, Talya flew to Oregon, spent the summer with her sister (the ass-kicking one who was now finishing her degree in Portland), took a full load of college courses, and completed the five GED tests leading to her GED certification. In September, she returned to Buenos Aires and enrolled in the very small American university there. She absolutely thrived in those tiny classes! She was at the center of attention as the only American in her U.S. History class, had her essays worked over with a fine-toothed comb by her Harvard-educated English Composition professor, fell in love with psychology in her intro class taught by an Argentine woman, spent hours in a biology lab with only eight other students in it, and delighted in the discussions in her comparative religion course taught by an animated Hungarian professor.

At the end of that year, she was offered a nice scholarship and grant package and transferred as a junior to a private university in upstate New York. Within days of her arrival, she had a job as a teaching assistant and was featured in a write-up in the college newspaper. She was 17 years old.

I realize that this is not a "normal" path for a teenager, and I can assure you that there were many, many times when my husband and I questioned whether we were doing the right thing by letting her shoot ahead. Time after time, we had to refocus our attention on her needs rather than our fears. We had many conversations with her about what she wanted for herself, and it was clear that she had really learned to trust her instincts about what "felt right" to her. We knew that this was an extremely important skill – the one most likely to allow her to make choices for a fulfilling life at every age – and that it was imperative that we give her the chance to practice it.

As a result, we watched her transformation from a shy, quiet, eager-to-please 14-year-old into a confident, bilingual young woman only too happy to defend herself and her ideas in any setting. She continues to be passionate about learning in Argentina – she spent a summer doing an independent study in Buenos Aires and is considering attending graduate school there. And she has found love – her boyfriend is a 21-year-old Argentine law school student.

What if we had allowed our fego (fueled by criticism from friends and family) to prevent us from moving abroad when Talya was 14? What if we had homeschooled Talya in Mexico? What if we had made her stay in high school in Buenos Aires? What if we had prevented her from starting college courses at 16? What if we'd said no to the GED or spending a summer taking college classes in Oregon, or felt she was too young to transfer as a junior to a college in another hemisphere at 17? There were so many points at which we could have chosen to block her progress, but we tried to focus on what mattered most: how she *felt*, what she *needed*, and how we could parent from a place of *pure love* rather than fear and ego. I am sure she would have done just fine spending four years in high school and four years in college, but our willingness to put our fego on a high shelf allowed her to leapfrog over her peers and get a personalized and exhilarating education on her own terms and timelines.

BECOMING BOLD PARENTS

Though it may be easier to fix things than to watch our kids struggle, we have to be strong enough to allow them to succeed – or fail. Bold parents learn that there is a dramatic difference between being supportive and solving our kids' problems for them. Our children develop confidence when we 1) encourage them to handle things on their own and 2) give them a chance to be successful without our assistance. Being bold as parents allows us to raise bold young adults; when we become wise mentors who give our kids opportunities to discover more about themselves and the world around them, we enable them to develop trust in their own instincts and their ability to navigate with confidence.

The key to becoming a courageous parent is to pay attention to those moments when fear and ego are guiding your behavior and make a conscious shift to focus on your child rather than yourself. Whenever you are faced with a challenge that stirs up these emotions inside you, pause and ask yourself these three questions:

1) What is my child *feeling* right now?

2) What does my child *need* right now?

3) What will happen if I offer *calm parental support* – focused attention on my child's needs for learning and growth – rather than allowing my own fear, ego, frustration, or the need to be "right" guide my response in this moment?

As parents, we won't always be paying attention to the right things. We get distracted. We get upset. We get just plain *tired*. And when we do, it's easier to just say no to our teenagers' requests for more freedom and discovery rather than deal with our own reluctance to let go.

You won't get every decision or comment just right. That's okay. The key is to practice, to pause when you need to, and to always recognize and reward yourself for those moments when you manage to give fego the slip.

Be kind to yourself (and proud of yourself) as you encourage your children to take steps toward independence. It's the hardest – and most courageous – thing a parent can do.

The Courage to Become Your Own Parenting "Expert"

Melissa Stanton

Melissa Stanton is the author of *The Stay-at-Home Survival Guide: Field-tested Strategies for Staying Smart, Sane, and Connected While Caring for Your Kids*. Prior to becoming a stay-at-home mother of three (including twins) in a suburb of Washington D.C., Melissa was a senior editor at *LIFE* and *People* magazines in New York. Her articles have appeared in *The New York Times, Glamour,* and *Brain, Child,* among other publications and Web sites. Having returned to the "work outside the home" workforce, Melissa is preparing a guide for at-home moms seeking paid employment. Visit with Melissa at www.RealLifeSupportForMoms.com.

The Common Sense Book of Baby and Child Care, by pediatrician Benjamin Spock, made its debut in 1946. This parenting how-to guide has sold more than fifty million copies worldwide and is among the most popular books of all time.

Through his book, Dr. Spock provided parents (or, at the time, primarily mothers) with the practical instruction manual many had wished for. And he did so in defiance of the standard child care practices of the day, which rigidly held to such dictates as *picking up a crying baby will spoil the child, children should be toilet-trained by a prescribed age,* and *infants should not be fed on demand.* Instead of ordering and scolding moms, Dr. Spock empowered them with assurances: "You know more than you think you do" . . . "Don't be afraid to trust your own common sense" . . . "Take it easy, trust your own instincts." Critics deemed his advice too permissive.

Dr. Spock's guidance has helped countless mothers and children, and his commercial success has helped inspire the dizzying array of child care and parenting books published since then. While access to parenting information is essential, the barrage of content – and opinions – can be overwhelming. Too often, instead of trusting their instincts, mothers today question their parenting skills and are questioned about them.

I crossed paths with Dr. Spock in 1987. He was in his eighties and spending much of his time sailing the Caribbean with his much younger, second wife. I was a 22-year-old editorial assistant at *Redbook* magazine, where Dr. Spock wrote a monthly child care column. Although I knew very well despite my young age that Dr. Spock was not to be confused with Mr. Spock of "Star Trek," I did wonder why an octogenarian grandfather was the parenting columnist for a magazine geared toward multitasking women trying to juggle the needs of career, family, and self. (Interestingly, even though Dr. Spock passed away in 1998, parenting advice is still being dispensed under his name at DrSpock.com).

A similar disconnect struck me years later, when I was a stay-at-home mother. I had left my career as a magazine editor due to my husband taking a job in Maryland, and for a too-long stretch we had a commuter marriage during which I spent my weekdays alone in our suburban New Jersey home with a preschooler and infant twins. While I was watching a morning news show one day, an especially primped and polished parenting magazine editor (who doubled as the program's "parenting expert") appeared for a segment about something related to rainy day fun for parents and children. As I watched this woman, I thought about the senior-level editors I had known at various parenting and women's magazines. Each worked full-time and their children were cared for by nannies or stay-at-home spouses. I was essentially working 24/7 at the beck and call of three small children, watching this magazine editor whose professional job was to tell me how to spend a day at home with my kids.

I'm not demeaning her parenting skills and devotion, or that of anyone in the parenting media. There's no reason to think that these men and women aren't great parents, and I also know full well that writers and editors often create quality content about subjects with which they have no hands-on experience. But my glimpses behind the curtain made me realize that the parenting "experts" – who run magazines, appear on television, write how-to books, and as doctors care for children or as academics study them – are often put on too high a pedestal. It reinforced to me the importance of being open-minded to information and ideas but not being dictated by what the ubiquitous "they" say. In other words, the great and powerful Oz is just a person with a microphone, and Dorothy is smart, capable, and courageous. (P.S. You're Dorothy.)

THE COURAGE TO FAIL THE TEST

When I first became a parent, I read books in the *What to Expect* series, but I didn't obsess and agonize about who my parenting guru would be. (Am I a Penelope Leach mom? Or a Dr. Brazelton parent?) I was reassured in my casual approach midway through my pregnancy when my friend Justine (not her real name) asked whether my husband and I had decided on "a discipline method."

Also pregnant, Justine had read that a specific child discipline strategy needed to be selected, and she somehow got it into her head that the discipline plan should be launched and ready to go on Day One. (Did she think her newborn would need a time-out?)

Later, as Justine started looking for child care so she could return to her job, one of her expectations was that the caregiver would use the baby's nap time to read child care and child development books and magazines. (I promise you, I'm not making this up.) In her interactions with other moms and caregivers, Justine was judgmental of people who, in her view, weren't as cautious and responsible as she was. Although she returned to her career after her child was born, she considered herself to be a more devoted and protective parent than many of her stay-at-home friends. For instance, a few years later, when I was on bed rest with twins and my husband was living out of state, Justine raised her eyebrows at me for allowing my son to be driven places by other moms. With a tsk-tsk tone, she told me that her nanny was the only person she and her spouse permitted to drive their daughters.

When I'm being gracious, I view Justine's parenting-by-textbook modus operandi and superior attitude as a mask for her extreme insecurity. She was likely a judgmental friend and a helicopter parent precisely because she wasn't courageous enough not to be. That happens, to both insecure and secure moms, because most every day, most every one of us thinks we're not doing a good enough job as a mother. We are told by "experts" what, as mothers, we should and shouldn't be doing for our babies and children.

Here's a little quiz to see just how good a mom you are. Give yourself 25 points for each rule you actually follow (or followed):

> A baby must weigh twenty pounds and be older than 12 months before using a forward-facing car seat

Babies should be breastfed for their first year of life

Children should start drinking from an open cup at 12 months of age, and unless being used at mealtime, sippy cups should only be filled with water

Children under age two should not watch television, and children ages three and older should watch no more than two hours of TV per day

How did you do? If you scored a perfect hundred, congratulations! Based on these four standards, you're on track to be a perfect parent – at least according to the American Academy of Pediatrics and the American Academy of Pediatric Dentistry.

If you didn't score one hundred, well, join the club – you may not be "perfect," but you fit in perfectly with most American moms. Here are a few areas where real life collides with "by the book" expectations:

The car seat. Many a mother converts her child into a forward-facing car seat before the child meets the precise safety criteria – e.g., 19 pounds and 13 months, as opposed to the 20 pounds and 12 months minimum standard. Are these women irresponsible mothers? No. They just know it's a lot more practical to have a child facing forward and within arm's reach than to be driving with a screaming kid they can't see or reach because he's facing backward.

Nursing. Breastfeeding timeframes vary based on each woman – her lactation, her child's nursing patterns and needs, the needs of her other children, and often, her return to the workforce. American women are told to breastfeed for a full year, but employed moms are rarely given one-year maternity leaves, nor is every employed mother able to pump and store her breast milk at work. The behavior of mothers is directed by policy and circumstance as well as choice.

The sippy cup. Few one-year-olds (or two- or three- or four-year-olds for that matter) can be trusted not to spill or fling a beverage in an open cup. Regarding the water-only rule for between meals: yes, as a means of cavity prevention, it absolutely makes sense that kids should not carry around a sippy cup of milk or juice for hours on end. But really, bonus points to the mom who actually trains her toddler to drink only water between meals or else sit at the table and drink from a regular cup every time he wants milk or juice.

Television. The only woman I've ever met who attempted to block her children from daytime TV entirely – while still having televisions in the house – was an employed mother who delegated the enforcement of the no-TV rule to her nanny. I'm embarrassed to admit how much television my kids watched as preschoolers. But should I be? When they watched TV, they were tuned in to educational shows like "Sesame Street" and "Blue's Clues." While no parent or caregiver should be sticking a child in a room with a TV and calling it a day, children's programming has come a long way since the smack'em-in-the-face-with-an-anvil humor of Wile E. Coyote and the Road Runner in "Looney Tunes."

While we're on the subject of mass media influences, unrealistic advice and expectations sometimes emanate from celebrity moms, whose status equips them, and seemingly their advice, with a greater impact. Television personality Kelly Ripa, in lamenting her own TV-addicted childhood, has been quoted as saying about her three children: "I want the kids to develop good habits. They're allowed to watch an hour of TV on weekends." During a television interview, Madonna explained that the televisions in her home are only for watching movies, which are generally rationed to one a week. Adhering to such hard and fast anti-TV rules is probably quite doable for Kelly Ripa and Madonna (both of whom have made millions from media careers) and other celebrity moms who more than likely have employees to care for their children and homes.

Parenting proclamations about behavior and routines are often set and promoted by people who, while highly educated and regarded in their field, generally don't spend days on end home alone with children. When as mothers we can't meet those standards, we feel bad about ourselves. A healthier model would be for us to recognize that there's the ideal world and the real world. Most mothers live in the real world and interact with real children.

THE COURAGE TO BELIEVE YOU'RE THE EXPERT

Louis XIV of France is said to have declared, "L'Etat, c'est moi." Essentially, "I am the State." When it comes to caring for their children, mothers need to develop confidence in asserting, "I am the Expert."

In an essay published in the online magazine *Literary Mama,* writer Denise Schipani revealed that to get her babies to actually sleep, she placed them face-down in their cribs, in clear violation of the Back to Sleep guidelines developed over the past generation to prevent Sudden Infant Death Syndrome (SIDS). The reason Schipani broke the rule? Her babies screamed on their backs but slept soundly on their bellies. The experience led her to conclude that a mother's judgment sometimes needs to trump what she's been told, even by her child's pediatrician. "When we put all our trust in the parenting gurus, listen to them slavishly rather than discriminatingly, we have less trust in our own budding parental wisdom," she writes. "Expert voices shouldn't drown out the inner voice that tells you what your baby wants, what your baby needs."

Debbie, a stay-at-home mother of three who responded to a survey for my book, *The Stay-at-Home Survival Guide,* shared a similar defy-the-expert experience: "When my daughter was two months old, her pediatrician told me to only nurse her every four hours. I tried to be a good mom and listen to the 'expert.' But my daughter was always hungry. When my boys were born, I nursed them on demand when they were newborns, then about every three hours as they got bigger. I soon realized I was the expert!"

My friend Lyn recalls how she knew and understood her son's needs better than the experts did. "I think back on my four-month-old first child, and me waving black-and-white cards and mobiles in his face incessantly, playing him classical music and massaging him daily according to the latest baby-care theories," she says. "This child was later diagnosed as being on the Attention Deficit Disorder spectrum. Who knew? Actually, I did. From infancy, he was easily overstimulated, and he struggled with auditory and tactile sensory overload. Something just didn't seem right, but all the books pointed me in the wrong direction."

What Lyn's son needed would now be considered a violation of the no-TV rule noted earlier in this chapter. "The only thing that worked was 'Sesame Street,'" she explains. "In the middle of the night, during the day, anytime all else failed. The experts say don't let little children watch TV, but 'Sesame Street' could soothe and calm this over-touched, overstimulated child. So he watched TV, a lot of TV, and I know now it was because of how his brain was wired that he craved it. Today, my son is an A+ student in a strong school. He's a driven athlete. He's kind, compassionate, and extremely polite. Thank goodness for 'Sesame Street.'"

Molly, another mom who answered my book survey, told me that when caring for her son, "I followed all the 'rules' for the first 18 months. Then I caved in and let him eat a french fry. Amazingly enough, the world did not come to an end, and I'm learning to be a more relaxed mom." (I often think fast food consumption is a universal dirty secret of parenting: most of us have fed our kids from a fast food joint – sometimes with frequency – yet none of us really wants to admit to doing so.)

Some women, through experience, confidence, or perhaps, a nonconformist attitude, are able to put the "experts" in their place from the get-go.

Before becoming a stay-at-home mother of three, Heather was a nanny and preschool teacher. "Many experts live in ivory towers rather than in the real world," she notes. "Stay-at-home mothers have no breaks and way too much to do, so on occasion we have to rely on the TV as a 'babysitter,' or feed our kids takeout."

Mother of four Ginny told me, "All of my children slept on their stomachs as infants, they all had cereal at three weeks, fruit at six weeks, and whole milk by nine months. None were breast-fed, they didn't go to preschool, they didn't have 45 'activities' that took their time away from just plain old-fashioned being a child." (And, adds Ginny, in reassurance to other less than pic-ture-perfect parents: "Although I cuss like a sailor, my children don't curse at all.")

"I like to think I have a Ph.D. in common sense, which I believe is far more useful," says Erin, a New Jersey mother of two grade schoolers. "Fast food occasionally. They never get out of car seats unless we're just down the street, or I don't have enough for the carpool, in which case I fasten everyone into seat belts. I think some parents follow rule books verbatim, but don't apply them to the right situations."

Dixie, whose children are now college-aged, provides some Zen-like advice to younger parents: "Your instincts are not per-fect, but they are as valid as many of the child-rearing philoso-phies that go in and out of style. Read, ask questions, trust those you respect – and trust your instincts."

MOTHER, KNOW THYSELF

Parenting, like baking, is as much an art as a science. Just as there are many ways to make chocolate chip cookies, there are many ways to care for and raise children. While really bad bakers will make really bad cookies, a vast variety of cookie recipes will turn out just fine, even though some involve using a mix, some start from scratch, and some require all-organic ingredients. Similarly, while there are, without a doubt, many really, really bad parents in the world, the rest (who may range in quality from adequate to exceptional) are getting the job done in their own ways.

As your own parenting expert, you need to establish your own constellation of parenting priorities – which you might also call your "touch points" or "deal breakers" – without being overly concerned about less vital issues, such as what your mom will say about your choices, what your neighbor does, or what the latest trend dictates. Just because the women on your block are making their own baby food, using "elimination communication" instead of diapers, or practicing the Ferber method of letting their babies self-soothe themselves to sleep doesn't mean you need to do the same. But it can be hard to buck trends and ignore peer pressure. When I was expecting my first child, I started checking out the child care solutions used by my friends. I quickly discovered that when it came to child care, some of my friends and I had very different priorities and deal breakers. While a few of my pals had nanny arrangements I envied (and still envy), others placed their children in care situations that I, for various reasons, found extremely unappealing.

To maintain our friendships we needed to not malign one another's child-related choices, whether the selections were about sitters, doctors, activities, or routines. That said, keeping the peace with other moms and being respectful does not mean everything and anything goes. If a child is being hurt, neglected or put in a potentially dangerous situation (think Britney Spears behind the wheel of her SUV with her baby on her lap), courtesy and tolerance be damned in favor of honest communication and, sometimes, intervention.

The boundaries of your own comfort zone, and your deal breakers, will change with time. My husband and I were religious about cuddling with our toddler son at his bedtime to read a book or just talk. When our twin daughters arrived, I was a weekday single parent. The nightly storytime dropped from my constellation of priorities. Although I felt guilty any time I saw a public service announcement telling me to read to my child every day, my solo juggling act controlled my reality. Knowing how to set your own (realistic) expectations and deal breakers is a good lesson to learn early. As every parent of older children and teens knows, the realities of their lives will someday require that you – and your kids – be very clear about your priorities. A time will come, if it hasn't already, when you'll have to say something along the lines of, "I don't care that Connor's parents are letting him skip school to go to the beach, you can't."

THE COURAGE TO BE COURAGEOUS, BUT CAUTIOUS

Today's parents are often accused of being ridiculously overprotective. But before passing judgment, we need to acknowledge that, sometimes, very bad things do happen. And violence, or perceived violence, especially when it's close to home, can cause parents to hover, even when they don't want to. Are these moms and dads being paranoid? Or are they being practical? The answer to both is yes.

In many ways, childhood is both safer and more dangerous than it was a generation ago. For instance, car seats, seat belts, and bicycle helmets help prevent injuries, but there are more cars on the road today than in the past, and those cars are moving at faster speeds. Unlike in my own youth, when parents didn't seem to worry much about sexual predators, parents today aren't as clueless (or in as much denial). However, since predators can now access children through the Internet, physical proximity is no longer the only risk factor.

Other changes have inspired escalated hovering. While a mother might allow her own kids to horse around in their fenced backyard while she's inside, it's harder for her to do when other children are visiting; in an age of liability, few moms want to be caught not watching the children playing in their yard, especially if it has a swing set, trampoline, or pool. Main Streets and small downtowns have been replaced by big-box retailers and strip malls. It's one thing for a child to walk a few blocks on a sidewalk past other homes and local businesses to the ice cream shop; it's another for that child to venture alongside a six-lane commercial thoroughfare with no sidewalks and then walk through a vast, asphalt parking lot to buy ice cream from a gas station mini-mart freezer.

Sometimes, children do move about in the world on their own, which was the case when journalist Lenore Skenazy let her nine-year-old son, Izzy, ride the New York City subway alone. An article Skenazy wrote about Izzy's self-motivated foray into independence landed her on the *Today Show,* where host Ann Curry introduced her by asking viewers, "Is she an enlightened mom or a really bad one?"

As a former New Yorker, I know what Skenazy did wasn't as bad as it may appear. Children in the city routinely use mass transit to get to school and activities. By day, the subway and buses are busy and populated with people who will help a youngster or, for that matter, a tourist, in need. Additionally, children can be in constant contact with parents via cell phones, and in this particular case the child was a savvy New Yorker who was comfortable navigating the transit system on his own.

I'll admit that I occasionally leave my 11-year-old inside our suburban home on his own while I run a nearby errand. I even let him walk without me from his school bus stop to our house. Do I have angst about it? Yes, I do. I play tug-of-war with myself between my desire to protect my son and my duty to help him develop the independence he wants and needs. It takes courage not to hover.

THE COURAGE TO BE HONEST ABOUT MOTHERHOOD – AND NOT "SPIT IN THE AIR"

If we're going to be our own parenting experts, we need to be honest about our roles as women and mothers. We are told, and typically believe, that motherhood is a blessing. But this oversimplification of motherhood plays right into the double standards we have for women as parents. As women, we're suspect if we don't have children, and as mothers, we're criticized for having children but remaining in the workforce, and for leaving the workforce to care for our children. We're told – and often believe – that our greatest fulfillment comes from our children and that we should love everything about being a mom.

With these conflicting expectations, all women "lose." Childless women often feel defensive about not being moms. Employed moms feel rotten for going to work – and for wanting to go. Stay-at-home moms feel like failures for leaving the workforce – and rotten for sometimes wanting to get away from their kids. Women routinely say that being a mom is the best thing that ever happened to them, but, according to Betsey Stevenson, co-author of the research paper "The Paradox of Declining Female Happiness" and an assistant professor at Wharton University, "Across the happiness data, the one thing in life that will make you less happy is having children." As she was quoted in Maureen Dowd's *New York Times* column: "It's true whether you're wealthy or poor, if you have kids late or kids early. Yet I know very few people who would tell me they wish they hadn't had kids or who would tell me they feel their kids were the destroyer of their happiness."

We love our kids (yes, we love 'em!), but we're afraid to admit that they are a part of our happiness rather than the entirety of it. We love our children, but we might also love having a career. We love our children, but we also love having time on our own, and time alone with our spouses, partners, and friends. Men are allowed to be fathers and so much more. The same should be true for women. It isn't unreasonable to think that the so-called Mommy Wars are waged because by demeaning someone else's choice or circumstances, we can feel better about our own. Motherhood is too often treated as a spectator sport, with women on the field as its fiercest competitors. It's destructive to all of us when either side takes a hit.

Having now played on many sides in the larger battle (as an employed mom, stay-at-home mom, work-from-home mom), I feel I can relate to the inner battles many mothers experience. Regrettably, my own wisdom and empathy wasn't always present.

A few years before we had our first child, my husband and I were invited to lunch at the suburban home of college friends I'll call Dan and Patty. When we arrived around noon after a nearly two-hour, traffic-filled, Sunday drive from the city, Patty, a stay-at-home mom to the couple's three children, was still in her pajamas. Dan was mowing the lawn. Their baby needed a diaper change. The older children, haphazardly dressed in stained clothes, were playing in a toy-strewn living room. This did not look like a family that was expecting guests for lunch, except that they were. Our visit was at Dan and Patty's urging. Lunch eventually amounted to each of us slapping together a sandwich from the half loaf of white bread and cold cuts that Patty scrounged together from the refrigerator. I left that visit hungry, angry (about wasting a day out of my weekend), and disdainful of stay-at-home moms.

At the time, I was working more than full-time. Patty, I felt, didn't work. And because she wasn't employed, I believed that, at the very least, her house should be clean, her kids should be well-groomed, and when we arrived she should have been dressed and had a lunch ready for our visit. In my view, the fact that she didn't do any of those things meant that she was incompetent, and enormously lucky to have found a man willing to support and take care of her.

Roughly a decade later, I had become (yikes!) a stay-at-home mother of three. My once-impressive meal prep skills had diminished to a small menu of what my kids would eat. Many rooms in my house were toy-strewn. My kids weren't the most well-groomed.

I had spit in the air and it came back to smack me in the face. *Splat! Yuck!*

I had become "Patty."

I tell the tale about the visit because – no surprises with this grand observation – it's easy to judge and criticize and pontificate about *shoulds* and *shouldn'ts*. It's easy to have high standards when we're not actually the ones having to meet those standards. It's easy to make assumptions, and even feel superior, when we haven't walked the walk.

Unlike during that visit, I'm now sympathetic to the chaos of caring for a home and small children. I now know very well that women who leave the workforce to raise children are not incompetent or in need of a Prince Charming to support and take care of them. (In fact, it may be that men with stay-at-home wives are the "lucky" ones: they're lucky to have a partner who is able and willing to provide the full-time, hands-on care of their children and home, and they're lucky to be able to earn enough for their household to live on one income.)

When we lose our sense of empathy, we make snap judgments

or demand perfection of others that neither they nor we can achieve. For instance, when Justine (yup, her again) was pregnant, she considered mothers who didn't nurse to be bad mothers. Fast-forward to a post-partum Justine suffering from mastitis while her screaming, hungry newborn lost weight. Out came the bottles – for the good of everyone in the family.

It can be hard to imagine straying from our perfect expectations until reality intrudes on our fantasies. We all wish for smooth, uncomplicated childbirths, healthy children, strong family relationships and continued employment. But *any of us* could find ourselves in a situation that requires help and understanding from others to get by. This can happen on a major life level or a small day-to-day occurrence: we've all recoiled at the seemingly unhinged mom who screams at her child in public. But then, one day, we too snap from our own child's tantrums and from our frustration at being unable to complete a simple task without first accommodating our entourage. Experience brings awareness, empathy, and ultimately, wisdom. Perhaps the courage to be our own expert needs to be accompanied by the courage to let other parents be theirs.

Life is a journey with many paths, and it's a game in which the rules change. It's best to keep an open mind, trust in your own abilities and choices, and not spit in the air. Before feeling beaten down about not doing what all those parenting experts advise, consider where the child-rearing tips and standards are coming from – and be realistic about what's essential to your child's well-being and what you can actually achieve.

The most practical bit of parenting advice I ever heard came from a woman who answered a survey for my book. Wrote Elizabeth: "Before my first child was born I had asked my mom, 'How am I going to know what to do?' She told me, 'All you have to do is love him. He won't know that you've never done this before. You'll learn together.'"

The Power of Personal Significance for Kids of All Ages

Amy McCready

Parenting coach Amy McCready is the founder of Positive Parenting Solutions. Her online course empowers parents with the skills to permanently correct misbehaviors without nagging, reminding, or yelling. You can learn more at her Web site, www.PositiveParentingSolutions.com.

If you want your children to keep their feet on the ground, put some responsibility on their shoulders.

~ Abigail Van Buren, "Dear Abby"

Raising children is the most important job that we, as parents, will ever have. In addition to being wonderfully rewarding, joyous, and heartwarming, it's also amazingly frustrating, stressful, and maddening. Our job – in addition to meeting our children's everyday needs – is to raise self-sufficient and responsible young people. Our goal is to move our kids from dependence to independence and equip them with the knowledge and skills they'll need to be happy, healthy, functioning adults.

Achieving this goal requires that we maintain a big picture view of our children's eventual independent adulthood while we allow them to take small, structured steps down that path each day.

What goes through your mind when you read this list of "firsts"?

First evening you left your child with a babysitter
First day of preschool
First sleepover at a friend's house
First "boy-girl" party
First time your teenager is a passenger in a car driven by a peer
First time you drop your teenager off at college

Whether these are past or future events, most parents feel a certain level of discomfort and anxiety when thinking about these milestones.

When do you say yes and when do you say no? What is the *right* answer and what if you make the *wrong* decision?

The reality is that to reach our parenting goal of raising independent, capable young adults, we have to equip our kids with skills, and then be willing to let go in many situations.

Letting go requires courage. Not the courage to face imminent danger, but worse – the courage to allow our children to fail, to experience the consequences of their own actions, and maybe toughest, the courage to give away some our own power.

DEPENDENCE TO INDEPENDENCE

So how do we do that? Intellectually, we know our job is to help our children develop into completely self-sufficient young adults who can meet life's little challenges independently and resiliently, and most importantly, not move back in with us after they've left the nest.

But, time after time in my parenting classes, I hear successful, educated parents lamenting that their teenager is unmotivated, doesn't take responsibility for his actions, and is perfectly content to play video games all day long. I recently worked with a family in which both parents have advanced degrees and are highly successful in their respective fields. Yet, they can't understand why their very bright high school-aged son lacks motivation in school, doesn't want to participate in sports or extracurricular activities, and has no interest in finding a job. He prefers to spend his free time playing video games and surfing the Internet. Another family with ample financial means and three teenagers wonders why the children don't have the work ethic and motivation of their successful physician father. Mom is busy most days cooking for and cleaning up after her teenage children, ensuring that they want for nothing.

The common thread tying these stories together is parents – parents who spent the past fifteen to eighteen years doing things for their child that she could have been doing for herself, sheltering her from uncomfortable situations, and making sure she wanted for nothing. These well-intentioned parents overlooked the duty of fostering in their child a very important basic emotional need: *personal significance.*

BELONGING AND SIGNIFICANCE

Parenting involves meeting our child's physical and emotional needs. Their physical needs are fairly clear: keep them fed, dry, clothed, and safe. Meeting a child's emotional needs is somewhat less obvious.

Basic tenets of Adlerian Psychology state that children have hard-wired emotional needs for belonging and significance. *Belonging* refers to a child's sense of emotional connection to individual members of the family and understanding how he "fits in" to the overall family constellation. Parents can foster a strong sense of belonging by providing plenty of *positive* attention and spending daily one-on-one time to emotionally connect.

Significance refers to the child's perception of himself as capable, able to make a difference, contribute in meaningful ways, and make some of his own decisions. These perceptions help a child feel powerful in a positive way. For this reason, the terms *significance* and *personal power* – although they are not entirely synonymous – are often used interchangeably.

Belonging and significance are equally important components of emotional health; however, here I will focus on the importance of fostering significance.

DEVELOPING PERSONAL SIGNIFICANCE

We don't often think of our role in parenting in these terms, but our real "job" is to guide our children from being completely dependent on us to functioning independently in an adult world. To make the leap from dependence to independence, they must have a strong sense of personal significance.

Fostering personal significance in children should begin early. To a toddler, significance may mean that she can do some "grown up" tasks independently such as getting dressed, making her own bed, helping with simple steps in preparing a meal, and feeding the pets. These tasks contribute to her sense of accomplishment in mastering new skills and reinforce that she makes a difference in the family. She knows that her contributions are meaningful and contribute to the welfare of her household.

Allowing a young child to perform some of these tasks on her own can be anxiety-provoking to parents. It takes a certain degree of parental courage to give your child the responsibility to dress herself and not worry about what other parents or teachers are going to think when you drop her off at preschool in the plaid skirt, striped shirt, and ballet slippers she selected for herself.

It takes even more courage to not drive your fifth grader's math homework to school when she repeatedly leaves it at home. A mom in a recent parenting class arrived thoroughly distraught over the events of that morning. She shared that on the way to school, her son announced that he forgot his journal on the kitchen table. Mom had already informed him that remembering his journal was going to be *his responsibility* and that she would no longer rescue him. She knew she had to stand by her word, so in that moment, faced with his likely meltdown, the reality that her son would not be prepared for class, and the fact that the teacher would fully "expect" her to drive home and get the journal, she calmly said to her child, "That's unfortunate. What ideas do you have to make sure you remember your journal in the future?" That was a moment of courageous parenting! Although her son was frantic about going to school that day, mom contributed to her son's sense of significance because she didn't rescue him. She helped him understand that *he* is responsible for his own things and that *he* has control over how his day will unfold at school.

As Nancy Gibbs reported in her *Time* magazine article "The Growing Backlash Against Overparenting," the school principal of Belinder Elementary in Prairie Village, Kansas, instituted a "no rescue" policy "when she noticed the front-office table covered each day with forgotten lunch boxes and notebooks, all brought in by parents. The tipping point was the day a mom rushed in with a necklace meant to complete her daughter's coordinated outfit."

In the adolescent years, the perception of significance and personal capability continues to grow. Each year, the child is able to master more adult-like tasks, such as keeping track of his cell phone, doing laundry, and preparing meals, in addition to managing his schoolwork. He is willing to take on more responsibilities because he is confident in his skills, and he recognizes that his contributions truly make a difference for the family.

A father of a teenage boy shared that getting his son to help around the house was always a battle. That was, until Dad began fostering his son's significance by training him on aspects of their home-based business. They began with the bookkeeping functions and it blossomed from there. The more he *learned* to do, the more he *wanted* to do, and his sense of capability and significance soared. Dad reported that his son's sense of pride in his accomplishments with the business spilled over into his schoolwork and his willingness to help with other family tasks.

Even with my own children, they may grumble a bit when asked to mow the lawn or rake the leaves, but deep down, the feeling of significance is real in knowing they accomplished a "grown up" task and in knowing that they contributed to the family in a meaningful way.

WHO HOLDS THE POWER IN YOUR FAMILY?

Significance includes the perception of capability and making meaningful contributions to the family. These concepts are fairly intuitive to most parents. A somewhat more puzzling component of significance is *personal power* – the perception that one has some control or influence over what happens.

Parents are often perplexed by the notion of personal power. They'll say, "How can she need power? She doesn't even know the meaning of the word *power*."

The concept of personal power to a toddler is similar to that of an adolescent or an adult. It is the idea of free will – having some dominion over your life and being able to influence, at least to some degree, what happens in your day. Fostering personal power in your child takes courage. It requires that we let go of some of our parenting power so the child can assume some of his own power.

While a child may not yet intellectually understand power, she is hard-wired with a need for it. This need begins in infancy and continues throughout life. An infant will instinctively fight back if an adult tries to restrain her. A toddler will stomp his feet and boldly say, "I do it!" when a parent steps in and tries to do something for the child that he is capable of doing himself. An irritated teenager will roll her eyes or sigh loudly when her helicopter parent tries to micromanage.

A toddler has real, legitimate power in three areas – eating, sleeping, and pottying. As hard as we may try, we can't "make" our toddlers eat, sleep, or poop! Therefore, these are the three areas where parents most often experience power struggles with toddlers. When young children battle us in these areas, it's their way of saying: "You can't make me! I'm not going to eat/sleep/ potty just because you want me to!" These power struggles are a toddler's way of telling us that they need more personal power.

We can foster a child's need for personal power by giving her more choices – more opportunities to make decisions, such as picking out her own clothes, choosing between two cereals in the morning, deciding if she wants to climb into the car seat by herself or be placed in the car seat, or choosing whether she would rather help set the table or tear lettuce for the salad. These are all examples of a young child exercising some control over her world in positive ways.

Imagine the same toddler with a parent who doesn't recognize the importance of personal power: "Okay, it's time to get dressed – here are your pants and shirt . . . it's time to eat, your Cheerios are ready . . . come here, let me put you into the car seat . . ."

Without the ability to make some of her own decisions and

control some aspects of her day, the toddler is likely to complain about the clothes you selected, dawdle on her way to the breakfast table, scream for Froot Loops instead of Cheerios, play "dead man flop" as you try to get her into her car seat, or all of the above!

I regularly get calls from parents wanting to know how to put an end to the temper tantrums, morning dawdling, and back-talk. These parents haven't learned that toddlers need opportunities for personal power. The negative power-seeking behaviors that parents so desperately want to eliminate are merely the child's way of saying, "I need some power of my own!"

I always remind parents that toddlers *will* get their power one way or another. We can either help them experience power in positive ways that are safe, sanctioned, and age appropriate, or we'll pay for it with tantrums, back-talk, refusal to cooperate, and a host of other negative power behaviors.

As children get older, there are even more opportunities to foster personal power in positive ways. Age-appropriate decision making may include choosing when to do homework, which family chores to do, which worship service to attend, which sport to try out for, or which colleges to visit.

Once again, if we don't *intentionally* work to foster the teen's perception of personal power by allowing him to make decisions and have some control over his life, we'll pay for it. The teen whose life is controlled by his parents may ignore his parents' requests, roll his eyes, slam doors, talk back, or throw tantrum-like outbursts. Or, his reaction may be more passive-aggressive, and he may do just the opposite of what his parents want.

Whether it's a toddler tantrum or teenage "attitude," the root cause is the same – the child's need for personal power as part of his overall need for significance. The child is determined to prove that "you're not the boss of me!" Parents need to have the courage to give power to their children so the children can be the bosses of some aspects of their own lives, thus developing their sense of significance.

FOSTERING SIGNIFICANCE REQUIRES INTENTION

Fostering a feeling of significance in children doesn't happen by osmosis; it takes work. In fact, parents today must be more *intentional* about fostering significance in their children than in generations past. It's not that kids are any different now – they still have the same genetic makeup. However, changes in society and in parenting styles have made it more challenging for kids to develop significance.

In past generations, children naturally developed a sense of personal significance out of their necessity to support the household. At a young age, they were expected to help with chores on the family farm or in the family business. On the farm, children may have milked cows, collected eggs, and maybe even sold farm products at a stand on the side of the road. In large families, older children cared for younger siblings, and everyone performed household tasks. Or, in the family restaurant, for example, they may have filled salt and pepper shakers, wiped down tables and chairs, and folded napkins. They worked side by side with older relatives and became competent in a wide range of important tasks. They knew they were making a difference and contributing to the family's success. Without the children's help, the farm or business operation would be impaired or could not function altogether. Today, our economy has changed so that it no longer provides built-in opportunities for children to contribute as they did in the past, and as a result, children lack a sense of importance within the household.

Few families today still operate a family farm or business. Our progression from a producer society toward a consumer society has taken a toll on the number of meaningful roles available to children as they grow and learn to become productive adults. Many of the jobs done by children in previous generations are now hired out: car washing, yard work, housecleaning, meal preparation, etc. While these conveniences make our lives easier and are likely here to stay, we must recognize that they rob our children of the opportunity to make valuable family contributions.

Because there are fewer *naturally* occurring opportunities for our children to develop a sense of significance, our challenge is to engineer meaningful ways for children to contribute so they genuinely feel capable, needed, and powerful. Guiding them from dependence to true independence requires that we be intentional about the process.

Although this takes a lot of work on your part, it's worth the effort to watch your child's confidence grow as he masters new skills. You'll find great joy in seeing the look of contentment on his face because his opinions were considered in an important family decision. And all your efforts to become a more effective parent will pay off when your daughter wants to hang out with you because she feels listened to and respected.

Not only do we have to be intentional about creating an environment that fosters significance, but we also have to be courageous enough to give up our own power to empower our kids.

At this point, you might be asking, how much power do I have to give up? How much is too much? Should I give in to every request for power?

Let's first look at this from a 30,000-foot view.

POWER AND THE PARENTING CONTINUUM

Psychologist Diana Baumrind, in her 1967 research, identified styles of parenting based on communication style, level of nurturing, and discipline strategies. The parenting styles described in her research can be placed on a continuum ranging from permissive on one end to excessively strict (authoritarian) on the other.

Permissive parenting demonstrates little regard for limits, structure, or a clearly defined system of consequences. The permissive parent is less likely to set expectations for behavior and hold the child accountable for her actions. If limits are set, they are quickly abandoned for expediency or the desire to not disappoint the child.

Parents on the permissive end of the continuum hold very little of the power, allowing the child to do as he wishes and make most of his own decisions without parental guidance or coaching. Ordinarily, the opportunity to make a lot of decisions would contribute to a child's sense of personal power and contribute to his overall perception of significance. However, parents who operate with a permissive parenting style typically don't provide the coaching and framework to support the decision-making process. Therefore, if the child makes a poor decision, there often isn't a system of consequences or accountability that helps the child learn to make a better choice in the future.

At the opposite end of the parenting continuum, authoritarian parents hold and keep the majority of the power. They make most of the decisions, and enforce a rigid system of rules with very clear punishments for transgressions. Such parents operate according to the philosophy, "It's my way, or the highway – and they'll thank me for this later."

Children raised in authoritarian homes have little input in family decisions or the course of their own lives, and as a result, they often lack skills in decision making, problem solving, and judgment. If children are rarely given opportunities to make decisions and experience the consequences of their choices, how do they ever learn the difference between appropriate and inappropriate choices? Consequently, it's common to hear of young people raised by excessively strict parents who "went wild" the first time they experienced the freedom of living away from home and often experienced painful consequences associated with their choices.

THE PROBLEMS WITH PERMISSIVE AND AUTHORITARIAN PARENTING

Permissive parents may think they are doing their child a favor by providing her with boundless freedom, and authoritarian parents may think they are helping to build their child's character by punishing him when he fails to meet their high standards. However, both ends of the spectrum are examples of fear-based parenting styles. Permissive parents lack the courage to set and enforce limits that may make the child unhappy in the short-term. A permissive parent would rather be a "friend" in the short-term rather than courageously hold the child accountable for her behavior and help her learn an important, enduring lesson.

Excessively strict parenting operates from a foundation of fear as parents hold on to power with a vice-like grip. Parents make the rules without family input or buy-in. If the child doesn't obey the rules and structure, he is punished. Parents on this end of the continuum assure themselves they are doing the right thing by using punishment, which employs blame, shame, or pain to force the child to conform to established behavioral expectations. To the strict parent, it's easier to say no to everything and remain in control than courageously say yes and risk potentially having to clean up a mess or pick up the pieces when the child makes a mistake. Unfortunately, this approach typically backfires in the long run. Children who are raised in excessively strict homes and subjected to *blame, shame, and pain* punishment may initially comply, but may act out with revenge behaviors down the road.

PENDULUM PARENTING

One thing worse than a permissive or excessively strict parent is one that swings back and forth from one end of the continuum to the other – the "pendulum" parent. Pendulum parents vacillate their parenting style depending on the tone of the family at the time. They usually begin with setting reasonable limits and appropriate consequences. Then, as family life gets crazy and they become exhausted, they lack consistency in following through on the consequences. Eventually, everyone forgets what the rule and consequence were in the first place. Misbehavior begins to escalate in a number of areas and the parents then decide it's time to "crack down." *BAM!* Now they've switched over to the authoritarian end of the parenting continuum. Let's face it – we've all done this at one time or another. But this pendulum approach is confusing for kids and doesn't contribute to a strong sense of significance and personal power.

POSITIVE DISCIPLINE – A MORE COURAGEOUS APPROACH

We don't have to choose between permissive and authoritarian parenting styles. We can combine the positive elements of *both* to provide freedom within limits. This is the cornerstone of Positive Discipline parenting, which combines a framework of clearly defined limits with age-appropriate freedom.

It requires courage to give the child freedom to make choices. It takes courage to accept that the child may not make the right choice, resulting in a painful lesson or consequence, and it takes courage to hold the child accountable for her behavior by implementing the applicable consequence. It takes courage to bring children into family decisions when appropriate and to compromise on how *you* want things to be done. And it takes courage to sometimes say no. These courageous actions describe the Positive Discipline parenting approach.

Parents following the principles of Positive Discipline are willing to give up short-term popularity with the child and their own personal prestige to ensure a long-term positive outlook for their family. Children raised by parents who operate by allowing freedom within limits develop a strong sense of significance. They grow up feeling capable, aware of their contribution to the welfare of the family, and knowing that their choices have a direct influence on their life.

GIVE POWER TO EMPOWER: THREE STRATEGIES FOR FREEDOM WITHIN LIMITS

Now that we've explored the concepts behind our behavior as parents, let's look at specific changes we can make to foster our children's feelings of personal significance.

Empowering our children with a strong sense of personal significance requires that we share a portion of our parental power with our kids, in developmentally appropriate ways. The three strategies discussed below embody the Positive Discipline approach and give positive power to children.

Provide kids with more positive choices. Children of all ages want to make decisions that affect their lives. Give away some of your parental power by offering age-appropriate choices within limits. Even a toddler can respond to choices such as: "Do you want to use the yellow towel or white towel?" or "Do you want your black shorts or the blue ones?" Elementary-aged kids can decide between options like: "Do you prefer to do your homework before or after snack?" or "Would you rather set the table or clean the dishes?" And for a teen: "Would you rather pick up your sister from soccer practice or get your brother from his play date?" Giving the child choices in the morning, after school, and evening provides opportunities for him to make real decisions throughout the day. As older kids successfully follow through on responsibilities such as homework, they can earn more autonomy over how and when they meet those responsibilities. Note that even if the choices given are related to work that needs to be done, or family obligations, the choices are always presented as proactive, positive options, never threats or ultimatums. Each time a child makes a decision, she feels a boost of positive power and significance. Each decision is an opportunity to have dominion or influence over some aspect of her life and as a result hones her decision-making and judgment skills.

Involve kids in family decisions and problem solving. Let go of some parental power by finding opportunities to bring children into family decisions. Involving children in the decision-making process boosts their significance and teaches important life skills. Identify areas where kids can be involved in *real* family decisions, and be sure to articulate the limits associated with those decisions. For example:

> "We can afford to spend thirty dollars on eating out this week. Let's decide as a family where we'll go."
>
> "We're driving to visit Grandma next month and can spend one extra day sightseeing. Let's decide as a family what stops we want to make along the way."
>
> "We've been having a problem with remembering to feed the fish. Let's work together to come up with a solution."

Empowering children to be part of family decision making and problem solving increases their sense of personal significance, ensures buy-in to the decisions, and teaches critical life skills that will serve them well into adulthood.

Give kids responsibilities and hold them accountable. One of the core child guidance principles of Adlerian psychology, the foundation of Positive Discipline, is to never do for a child what she can do for herself.

Parents are always amazed at how independent and self-sufficient their children are at school and frequently ask, "Why doesn't she do that at home?" Well, the reason is . . . we don't give them the chance! We underestimate how capable our children *could be* with a little training and encouragement, and as a result, we do things for them.

When we do things for our kids or assume responsibility for things that they are perfectly capable of doing, we rob them of the opportunity to become self-sufficient and to contribute in meaningful ways – the very definition of significance. To avoid this common parental pitfall, identify age-appropriate tasks that your child can do to contribute in the family. Take the time to train your child on the step-by-step process of performing the task and then hold her accountable for doing it. For example, train an eight-year-old to pack his own lunch, being very specific about the process, and empowering him with the responsibility to pack it each day. Have the courage to not step in to ensure he cuts off the crusts "your way," and have the courage to not remind him to make a lunch or rescue him when he forgets it at home. Train your 13-year-old to do his own laundry. Again, be specific about the process and put the responsibility squarely on his shoulders. If he realizes that he forgot to wash his baseball uniform the night before a game, have the courage to empathize, but not rescue. Let the *natural consequences* of a child's action or inaction "do the talking" whenever possible. This means less nagging for you, and your children are more likely to learn by experiencing the natural outcomes of their actions. Believe me . . . this is going to be work on your part on the front end – but you and your children will see benefits beyond measure in the long run!

FINDING THE BALANCE

The hardest part of raising children is teaching them
to ride bicycles . . . A shaky child on a bicycle for the
first time needs both support and freedom. The realization that this is what the child will always need can
hit hard.
~ Sloan Wilson

Our job is to lovingly guide our children from complete dependence on us to being fully independent, responsible, resilient, and
resourceful. (Oh . . . is that all?)

To do that successfully requires intention and courage. The
courage to bear the constant internal struggle that pits our overwhelming love for our kids and desire to shelter them from
discomfort and disappointment against our commitment to courageously empower them with a sense of significance and personal
power. There is a fine line between helpful nurturing and crippling
enabling, and we must learn to find and maintain the balance.

The courageous strategy of providing freedom within limits is
hard work and can be intimidating, but it is in the very best interest of our children. When we come to terms with letting go of
some of our parental power to empower our children, amazing
things will happen. Our kids will become more capable and self-
sufficient than we ever dreamed possible. The family will feel like
a team with everyone working together for the common good.
And, best of all, *they'll want to be with us*. They'll openly communicate with us because they feel respected. We'll have fun as
a family and we'll truly enjoy parenting, not merely survive it!
What could be better than that?

I'm Worried I Worry Too Much, But How Do I Stop?

Jamie Woolf

Jamie Woolf has a master's degree in industrial/organizational psychology and over 25 years of experience providing consulting to business leaders. Based on her work inside dozens of organizations, she founded The Parent Leader, a firm that conducts workshops to help parents combine self-awareness and leadership skills to transform their daily parenting challenges into desired results. Jamie is also the author of *Mom-in-Chief: How Wisdom from the Workplace Can Save Your Family from Chaos* and the co-founder of Pinehurst Consulting, an organization development consulting firm. She lives in Oakland, California with her husband and two daughters. To learn more about The Parent Leader's services and resources, visit www.MomInChief.com.

We parents are a bunch of worriers. It's well-documented. We rescue, overprotect, and hover. The good news is, we're on to us. We worry that we worry too much. Intellectually, we know that abductions are rare, but emotionally, that primal fear can grip our hearts. We can cite the rhetoric: if we don't let our kids struggle a bit and strengthen their resilience muscles, they'll crumble once they leave their protected childhood bubble.

But parents are a stubborn bunch. A few statistics and a barrage of media attention about modern-day parental anxiety doesn't stop us from continuing to do what we rationally know might actually be harming our kids. So how do we quit the worry habit?

First, here's the worry medley that flowed, without a moment's hesitation, from the mouths of a group of my parent friends when I asked them what worries were on their minds:

> Are my children not eating enough fruits and vegetables? Not eating enough in general? Are they too social? Will they drink alcohol and drive? Will he ever be able to go to sleepovers without those creepy pull-ups for "big boys"? Will I die before they reach adolescence? What message does my unhappiness at work send to my son? Will video games turn their brains to mush? Why doesn't he love to read? Am I damaging them by talking on the phone to friends while they play by themselves? Will Hannah Montana turn her into a sexualized teenager? Will they graduate high school? Will they get into college? Do they have the right friends? Are they in enough activities or too many activities? Should I be giving them music lessons? Did I miss the window for teaching them a second language? Are they too fat? Too skinny? Will she have eating disorders? Is she reading too slow? Is she attending the right school? Do I spend enough quality time with them or do I work too much? Am I too intrusive or not intrusive enough? Am I strict enough or too strict? Am I damaging them by putting them in preschool too early? Has she led such a sheltered life that she will collapse at the first sign of a real bump in the road? Will she be happy?

There are too many drunk drivers, earthquakes, sexually transmitted diseases, drugs, inappropriate Internet sites, and trans fats to stamp out worry altogether. The question is, Do we *live* in the worry zone, or, when we start to get lost in worry, catch ourselves and shift to a more courageous mindset?

What can you do when every decision, big and small, feels rife with consequences that will affect your child from now to eternity? I've compiled a few simple parent leadership strategies based on hundreds of coaching conversations I've had with parents and business leaders alike facing anxiety-provoking dilemmas. By practicing these strategies, you'll more easily recognize when you're stuck in worry and find ways to shift your perspective so that you spend less time ruminating, blowing things out of proportion, and second-guessing yourself.

We'll begin by discovering your Parenting Mode and move on to examining how your mode runs amok when you worry. Here's the good news: every parent has their own personal style, or Parenting Mode, that showcases their strengths and inspires those around them. When you leverage your Parenting Mode, the fatigue of the job melts away and you feel deeply satisfied. You're no longer wracked with self-doubt, wondering, *Am I doing this right? Am I screwing up my kid?* You're no longer making short-sighted choices fueled by anxiety and faulty thinking; you're making choices that are aligned with your highest parenting priorities. You're connecting but not interrogating, you're guiding but not rescuing, and you're encouraging but not pressuring.

Here's the challenge: during times of stress and worry, each Parenting Mode is prone to its weaknesses rather than its strengths. Once you know your mode, you can think of it as shorthand to better understand how your natural strengths can backfire when you're stressed. After taking the quiz below, total your scores, discover your Parenting Mode, and see how it can run amok in ways that may obstruct your effectiveness.

THE PARENT LEADER QUIZ

Instructions. Rank the choices (*a, b,* and *c*) below each statement from *1* to *3*. Place a *3* next to the answer that *best* characterizes you in your parenting role, a *2* next to the answer that somewhat characterizes you, and a *1* next to the answer that *least* characterizes you. Be sure to rank all three choices. Don't overthink your responses. Be honest – don't just respond in the way you feel is socially desirable. There are no good or bad responses.

Remember: *3 best* characterizes you and *1 least* characterizes you. Respond in the context of your parenting role.

1) I most value for my child . . .
a) ____ Achievement
b) ____ Emotional connection
c) ____ Individuality

2) My most important role as a parent is to . . .
a) ____ Foster individuality
b) ____ Build close connection
c) ____ Unleash potential

3) I'm most likely to say to my child . . .
a) ____ Strive for success
b) ____ Be yourself
c) ____ Build healthy relationships

4) My top priority as a parent is to . . .
a) ____ Encourage intimacy
b) ____ Foster independent thinking
c) ____ Encourage growth

5) I most want my child to . . .
a) ____ Be emotionally aware
b) ____ Be true to self
c) ____ Seek challenge

6) My most common parental challenge is . . .
a) ____ Overreacting
b) ____ Pushing too hard
c) ____ Providing enough emotional support

7) As a parent, I tend to have little patience with . . .
a) ___ Conformity
b) ___ Apathy
c) ___ Insensitivity

8) As a parent, I can be . . .
a) ___ Competitive
b) ___ Over-involved
c) ___ Remote

Scoring. Transfer the number *(3, 2, 1)* that you wrote in each blank to the corresponding blank below. For example, if you put a *3* in the first blank, 1) *a,* then transfer that below so that 1) a: *3.* After you have transferred your rankings, add up the total score for each of the three categories. The category with the highest total score indicates your dominant parenting orientation.

Achievement	*Individuality*
1) a:	1) c:
2) c:	2) a:
3) a:	3) b:
4) c:	4) b:
5) c:	5) b:
6) b:	6) c:
7) b:	7) a:
8) a:	8) c:
TOTAL: _____	TOTAL: _____

Relationships
1) b:
2) b:
3) c:
4) a:
5) a:
6) a:
7) c:
8) b:
   TOTAL: _____

QUIZ INTERPRETATION

The mode with the highest total is your preferred style. This is the mode from which you get the most benefit, because it's where you do your best work and achieve your greatest rewards. Typically, one mode is least developed. This is an area for personal growth. This is also the area where you may run into struggles with a co-parent. You may have two scores which are close or tied. This means both modes are preferred and likely to be demonstrated depending on the circumstance.

It's important to remember that like any assessment, this is only meant to be a starting place to cultivate self-awareness and open up conversations about your approach to parenting.

ACHIEVERS PROMOTE ACHIEVEMENT

Ambitious, successful, and conscientious, Achievers see their most important role as inspiring achievement and growth. They raise the bar high, encouraging their child to stretch and continually seek new challenges. Achievers raise expectations and encourage children to reach higher levels than they would without direction.

Achievers' worry alert. You may get too caught up with your child's achievements, pushing your own agenda instead of accepting your child's interests and predispositions. Because you take pride in your own success, you may become judgmental or critical when your child doesn't demonstrate the same zeal for excelling. You may plan a jam-packed enrichment regimen even when your child shows resistance. Given your competitive tendencies, you may worry whether your child's preschool is challenging enough or wish your child were more like the kid down the street who pulls straight A's and wins piano competitions. When a child shares her academic struggles with her parent, the Achiever parent may naturally jump in with advice and solutions – let's get a tutor, you need to spend more time on homework, you need to organize your desk, no more TV until your homework is done – instead of listening *without judgment.* Your challenge is to think first about what is best for your child given her unique interests, personality, and passions, separating out your own personal hopes and dreams.

CONNECTORS BUILD RELATIONSHIPS

Connectors' central sense of parenting satisfaction comes from emotional connection with their child. They see their most important role as nurturing and expressing affection. They strive to ensure that each family member's needs are heard and supported. Connectors build strong bonds that make children feel valued, safe, and trusted.

Connectors' worry alert. As a Connector, you may rush in to protect or rescue. You may get overly involved in your child's emotional life, lose control of your emotions, or make shortsighted decisions to protect you and your child from pain. You need to resist the urge to pry into the private life of your children. You may feel you are showing interest, but healthy involvement can unwittingly turn into interrogating, prying, and invading privacy, which results in shutting communication down – ironically, creating exactly what you, as a Connector, fear most. For instance, a classic Connector reaction may be to talk to your daughter's teacher about a classmate who is excluding your daughter from recess games, even when your daughter asked you not to. Your challenge is to keep your emotions in check and allow your child to navigate difficulties on their own, resisting the urge to rescue, protect, or get overly involved.

LIBERATORS FOSTER INDIVIDUALITY

Liberators' central sense of parenting satisfaction comes from seeing their children making their own choices and discovering their own uniqueness. Liberators see their most important role as providing the room and the safety for their children to develop into unique, self-sufficient individuals. They strive to foster independent thinking. They're primarily concerned with backing off and leaving plenty of room for their child's individuality to flourish. They love to cultivate and honor each child's interests and choices.

Liberators' worry alert. When your child shows signs of trying too hard to fit in with peers, you may ridicule her or neglect to demonstrate empathy for her need to belong. For example, your child says, "I'm not wearing those glasses to school." You say, "Don't worry so much about what other people think," and the conversation shuts down. You may lie awake worrying about how to help your child combat the power of peer pressure. Wanting your child to feel independent and confident, you may get impatient when your child whines about missing you when you leave for a business trip. You may snap at her when she gets clingy in unfamiliar settings, and worry that she is timid or insecure. Your challenge is to recognize your emotional reaction and find ways to strike a balance between encouraging independence *and* providing support.

BIG-PICTURE PARENTING GOALS

Once you understand your Parenting Mode, the next step is to get clear on your big-picture parenting goals.

I begin most of my parenting seminars with the question, "What are your primary goals or core values at home?" Typical responses include:

I want to raise a self-confident child

I want my child to contribute to the greater good

I hope my children find work that is meaningful

I hope my children find relationships that are fulfilling

I want to help my child find out who she is meant to be in this world

Focusing on your big-picture goals transforms the burden of daily worries into something more uplifting. The challenge is to keep this mental picture in your mind when you find yourself stuck in the emotional quicksand of fear and worry.

My sister-in-law, Lian, has a compelling big-picture goal that helps her to be aware, not afraid.

I want my boys to be rough-and-ready, not hothouse flowers. That means teaching them to ride a city bus, read a train schedule, show up on time, carry their own gear. I want them to handle going off to college, bumming around Europe with a backpack, navigating a foreign city, showing up at work on the first day on time and ready to roll.

Being a parent brings endless anxieties. It's easy to lose sight of the bigger picture, but focusing on your goals can ease the worry. As you broaden your perspective beyond everyday concerns, worry's grip loosens – the challenge is to keep your bigger goals in your mind as you break up the sibling battles, insist that homework gets done, and find yourself getting swallowed up by worry.

To formulate your big-picture goals, begin by imagining that your children are grown. Reflect on the following questions and discuss them with your spouse or co-parent or a friend:

What do your children, as grown people, say about your
family's strongest values?

Which of your hopes for your children have been fulfilled?

What five qualities do they possess?

What qualities do they admire about you?

What big-picture parenting goals have *you* met?

The next parent leadership strategy is to *act* in alignment with
the big-picture goals you've just established.

The best leaders ask themselves, *What must I do today to support
my goals and my desired outcomes?* Big-picture goals drive success,
but they're hard to stick to, especially when we feel anxious. The
clearer your goals are in your mind's eye, the more likely you are
to behave in a way that supports them. Chart out specifics, enlist
support, recognize when you make progress, and don't beat yourself up when you fall prey to acting out of worry. Falling into the
worry zone is an inevitable hazard of the job. Remember, the key
is not to stay out of the worry zone altogether, but rather mini-
mizing *how long* you're stuck there.

CONNECTING ACTIONS TO GOALS

Is your big-picture parenting goal for your children to become
responsible and self-sufficient? With this goal vividly in mind,
you will be better able to catch yourself when you veer into your
worry zone, and to take corrective action to realign with your
goals. For example, acting from the worry zone, you may rush
back to school to deliver your child's forgotten homework instead
of allowing her to learn a little life lesson that her actions (forgetting her homework even after you reminded her) have consequences. I recently caught myself nagging my teenage daughter:

"Do you have your tennis shoes? How about your bus pass? Do you need money? Is your cell phone charged? Did you get your essay from the printer?" Aieee! However well-intentioned I may feel, the actual message I am conveying to my daughter is *You're forgetful, dependent, helpless.* She's none of these things. Once I got clear about my big-picture goal to foster her independence and self-confidence, I backed off. She forgot her tennis shoes the very next day and had to put up with a reprimanding PE teacher. Big deal. Lesson learned.

Do you want your child to experience the pleasure of freedom and self-confidence? Let her walk alone to her friend's house down the street. Do you want to foster your child's love of reading? When he's reading to you and you start to feel impatient as he stumbles over words, praise his progress and effort and take a breather. Do you want to strengthen your child's self-confidence? When she comes home complaining that she was teased, resist the temptation to go to school and manage the situation. Take a breath and then give her a strong message that you're confident she has the ability to handle it. You can problem solve with her in a way that helps her find her own solutions. Are you in power struggles over your son's messy room? Remind yourself that your big-picture goal is to build a nice heart-to-heart connection with your son, and close his bedroom door. Are you frustrated with your child's aimlessness? Knowing that you want to foster his ability to use his imagination and manage his own time, you may allow your son to wallow in his boredom for a while rather than rushing in with an agenda of parent-guided activities. Are you tired of chores not getting done and tempted to do them yourself? Take a breath, and remember your big-picture goal is to foster responsibility; persevere with chore assignments for the whole family rather than taking over the tasks yourself.

A WORRY ANTIDOTE

A good antidote to worry – and a powerful way to act in alignment with your big-picture parenting goals – is to pursue your non-parenting dreams. This may seem counterintuitive, but I've found it to be true in my experience talking with parents who have lost precious parts of themselves while busy taking care of the needs of others. In coaching leaders, one of the first lessons I teach is this: to perform your best and inspire the best in others, you need to step back from the pressure and nurture yourself. Whether we are running a company or a carpool, when we don't take a breather and focus on our non-parent or non-employee selves, our joy is too often displaced by feelings of resentment and pointless stress. How can we expect our children to pursue their dreams when we defer our own? Good parenting, like good leadership, is about modeling the behavior you want others to emulate. If you're like most parents, you want to raise a happy, self-respecting child who pursues her passions. One of the most powerful ways you can do that is to be a living example of a person who finds happiness in pursuing her own dreams. Furthermore, living your own dreams takes pressure off your kids to vicariously fulfill them for you.

When we're in the worry zone, we're irritable, moody, cautious, fearful, risk-averse, and critical, drawing conclusions instead of seeing the possibilities. Pursuing dreams opens us up to feel freer, happier, and more empowered – all important ingredients for being a good parent, not to mention a good role model.

What actions are you willing to commit to in support of your dreams?

PUTTING IT ALL TOGETHER: TAMING YOUR WORRY

Take a moment to answer the following introspective questions intended to help parents shed their worry. The point of this exercise is to help you come to a connect-the-dots moment in which you realize the liberation that comes from translating your self-knowledge and your big-picture goals into concrete actions. Included is a sample response taken from one of my workshops, modified to protect the parent's identity.

1) What current worry is on your mind?

> I'm worried that my son is not athletic. In fact, he's pretty clumsy and accident-prone. I worry that he will be excluded by other boys in his class and that he will be the butt of their jokes.

2) How is your Parenting Mode running amok in relation to your worry?

> I'm a Connector and so I tend to jump to the worst-case scenario, losing sight of logic, of reality! I can also get enmeshed, forgetting that he is a distinct person from me and that is a good thing. Sports made me happy as a kid, but my son is his own unique person.

3) Step back a minute: what is your big-picture parenting goal?

> My big picture parenting goal is pretty simple – to raise a happy child.

4) How can you discard the worry and take action in alignment with that goal?

If I step back from my emotions, I can see that my son is indeed happy. He has lots of friends. I don't think he worries much about not being an athlete. I worry that boys who aren't athletic have a harder time, but so far I haven't seen much evidence that he has a problem with it. My action: focus on all the activities my son enjoys – playing guitar, playing video games with friends, being in plays. Follow his cues to ensure I expose him to activities that match his interests. I may have loved sports as a kid, but my son is not me!

Knowing your Parenting Mode and how it can backfire is an important step in building self-awareness, a critical factor contributing to your effectiveness as a parent. Worries can wreak havoc, pulling you away from your more successful parenting behavior. When we're deluged with countless worries, it's easy to lose sight of the bigger picture. With a focus on big-picture goals and an understanding of your strengths and how they can backfire under pressure, you are better equipped to weather the inevitable worries parenting brings. There's no question that being an effective parent is a tall order when emotions run high (which is most of the time). But if you pause and go through the strategies outlined in this chapter, you're apt to have fewer sleepless nights and a lot more success raising happy, confident kids.

section three

Real-world Safety Skills for All

Sometimes it takes courage to send our kids into the world, and these days, thanks to the Internet, the world also comes to us in new ways.

Whether we are participating in the physical or virtual world, there are many safety skills that we all need to know. Unfortunately, we, as parents, are often bombarded with scary stories but are rarely taught the skills that we, and our children, need to stay safe. No matter how old our kids are, and whether or not they are having independent experiences yet, it's not too early to educate ourselves about these issues. After all, parents of even very young children make important judgments about child safety, such as whom to choose as a babysitter, how much direct supervision a child needs in a variety of situations, and what information is appropriate to share about their family online.

This section begins with an introduction to the personal safety skills kids need as they develop and their independence grows, presented by Irene van der Zande, co-founder and Executive Director of Kidpower Teenpower Fullpower International. This grassroots organization has had a major impact: over the past twenty years, Kidpower has taught personal safety skills to over 1.2 million people worldwide. As parents, we want to keep our children safe *and* foster their independence, but with all of the different ways that children can experience harm, these goals sometimes seem at odds with each other. But as Irene explains in "Kidpower: Skills for Safety, Skills for Independence," safety and independence actually go hand in hand. She introduces us to personal safety skills and effective ways to teach them to our kids (and learn them ourselves). The key to raising kids into independent, capable young adults is to help them develop the tools they need to navigate their world with safety and confidence.

Clearly, the Internet is here to stay and will continue to have a big impact on all our lives, especially those of young people who are growing up as "digital natives." Considering Internet safety, one point that may be counterintuitive to parents is that, just like physical safety, keeping children safe in the digital age begins at birth, long before kids actually participate on the Web. We need to think about what information we are sharing online, and keep an eye on what information others are sharing about us. For example, consider a Web site's terms of use and privacy settings before you fill out an online baby announcement that includes your child's full name, birthdate, and parents' names – this information could be misused to commit identity theft. Keep an eye on whether Grandma is sharing too many personal details about your family on her blog, and talk to her about it if necessary. Think critically about whether your school is posting too much personally-identifiable information on its public Web site.

Linda Criddle is an Internet safety expert who has seen the workings of cyberspace from the inside out. During her years as a Microsoft executive, she was an online safety pioneer for the whole company, including MSN, the Web portal now serving over six hundred million people worldwide each month. She understands predatory behavior, technical issues, and policy-based solutions. Now, as a consultant and educator, she applies her vast knowledge in her role as an independent consumer advocate. Despite the potential problems that can arise with the Internet, Linda emphasizes that it is a powerful tool that all of us should be able to use. The key to using email and the Internet safely is learning how to identify and avoid risks online, which she addresses in depth in "How to Say *Yes* to Your Kids' Online Activities." Although it requires a conscious effort to learn, the safety skill set that Linda presents can, with practice, become an automatic, ingrained part of a family's online habits.

Kidpower: Skills for Safety, Skills for Independence

Irene van der Zande

Irene van der Zande is the Executive Director and co-founder of Kidpower Teenpower Fullpower International, a nonprofit organization that has brought personal safety and confidence skills to over a million children, teens, and adults of many cultures across the United States and around the world. Since 1989, Irene has led the creation of the organization's curriculum, development of centers, and training of instructors, and has written extensively about personal safety. Irene is also the author of *1,2,3 . . . The Toddler Years* and co-author of the textbook *The Parent/Toddler Group*. To learn more about Kidpower's free articles, podcasts, and videos, as well as workshops, *Kidpower Safety Comics* and other print publications available for purchase, visit www.kidpower.org.

Kidpower was born from my passion as a mother to protect my children from harm while giving them the freedom and tools they needed to grow into joyful, independent adults – and fueled by the passion of countless other parents and caring adults to do the same.

This journey started over thirty years ago, when I was a new mother walking down the street carrying my tiny baby and experiencing a sense of vulnerability that I had never felt before. Overwhelmed with love, I cradled my baby, Chantal, in my arms and wondered how either of us was going to survive her growing up. Life seemed abundantly full of joy that I wanted to share with Chantal – and treacherously full of danger that I wanted to protect her from. I felt totally responsible for everything she did and everything that might happen to her and unsure whether I was up to the job.

One night, Chantal choked on her spit and my husband, Ed, and I were awakened by a strangled scream that got both of our hearts pounding. As soon as we picked her up, she quickly calmed down, but I couldn't stop shaking. I turned to Ed and wailed, "I should have stopped this from happening to her! I'm a terrible mother!"

Ed gently pointed out that Chantal needed to learn for herself how to breathe while she swallowed her spit, because as much as I wanted to, I couldn't do that for her. He reminded me that, even as a tiny newborn with both of her parents asleep in the middle of the night, our baby had been able to yell for help when she needed it – and that we had been there to help her.

As courageous parents, our challenge is to find the right balance between letting our kids grow up and keeping them safe while they do it. To do this, we need to understand what they are capable of, what problems they might face, how to give them the tools they need to deal with these problems, and when to do things for them or let them do things on their own.

Kidpower was inspired by my own search to find answers as a parent, especially after a disturbed man threatened to kidnap a group of young children in my care, including my seven-year-old daughter and four-year-old son, during an outing in 1985. Even though I stopped him by yelling to attract attention and help, this experience raised lots of questions for me about how to protect my children and teach them to protect themselves.

In 1989, I joined with many other parents, educators, law enforcement officials, and mental health experts to establish Kidpower as a nonprofit organization. Kidpower's goal was and is to prepare children, teens, and adults, including those with special needs, to become safer and more confident through successfully practicing "People Safety" skills – skills for taking charge of one's emotional and physical safety with people.

Here are some of the lessons we've learned, through working with more than a million people over the past twenty years, about how parents can prepare children to explore their world with safety and confidence.

ACCEPTING THAT THERE ARE NO GUARANTEES

Recently, in a parent education night, a mother asked me desperately, "How *old* is my daughter going to be before I get to stop worrying? I'm *so* tired of being so afraid!"

Her daughter was four.

With a great deal of sympathy, I had to give this worried mother some bad news: "My children are adults now and do a great job of taking care of themselves. But, I never get to stop feeling like their mom, and my heart still skips a beat any time I think of a possible threat to them! And do you know what? My parents are over eighty and I'm over sixty – and they *still* worry about me!"

Accepting that there are no guarantees helps me to regain my perspective and sense of calm as a parent. Uncertainty is a reality of life, and constant worrying about what might happen will just make everyone miserable without making anyone safer. Instead, we can learn to manage our anxiety by taking effective actions that will keep our children safe most of the time.

I am reminded of the words of philosopher Sir Francis Bacon, who said, "He that hath . . . children hath given hostages to fortune . . ." and those of author Elizabeth Stone, who said, "Making the decision to have a child . . . is to decide forever to have your heart go walking outside your body." Although Sir Francis was speaking of children as barriers to a man's worldly achievements, I choose to view his words differently. For me, his and Elizabeth Stone's words mean that those of us who are lucky enough to have children in our lives are all held in the grip of things outside of our control, and must, to some degree, surrender our children and ourselves to the occasionally dangerous fates of the world.

That's just the way life is. Letting our fears about these realities stop us from enjoying our own lives does not make our children safer. Letting our fear cause us to be constantly anxious and restrictive can make our children's lives more stressful and less enjoyable, but it won't make them safer.

I have learned so much from working directly with thousands of families who have taken Kidpower training. As one concerned mother told me, "I tried to protect my daughter, Ariel, from everything. I never let her climb up on a play structure for fear of falling. I didn't let her play in a swimming pool because of germs. And I kept her away from other kids and families who might stress her out too much.

"When she was almost eight, Ariel got terribly sick. As I sat in her hospital room, I thought about all the fun my fear had kept my child from having. When she, thankfully, got better, I decided to set my fear aside and take more risks. Ariel has broken her arm, gotten head lice, and coped with a bully. But her joy in doing new things has been worth it."

The reality is that, statistically, a child's biggest risk of being killed in the United States is from being a passenger in a car. However, by taking reasonable precautions such as using seat belts and car seats and not text messaging while we drive, we can reduce the risks and keep the benefits of using our cars. We can apply the same common-sense approach to other decisions we make for our children.

We need to accept that no matter how careful we are, bad things might happen that are simply out of our control. Yet, we should not let those possibilities rule our lives or unnecessarily curtail our kids' experiences. We want to take reasonable precautions and teach our children the skills they need to safely, confidently enjoy their lives, rather than living in an unnecessarily restricted, fearful bubble.

We want our children to see their lives as an adventure, rather than seeing uncertainty as a cause for worry and fear. When problems come up, we want our children to see themselves as explorers of life, overcoming challenges, not as victims of the unexpected. Kidpower gives families the skills they need to confidently approach life with safety and independence.

BEING PREPARED FOR CHANGE

Although change is a reality at any stage of life, children tend to change more quickly and suddenly than adults. For parents and caregivers of children, this means that we are constantly readjusting the parameters for the supervision and limits we impose on our children to protect their well-being.

I will never forget when Chantal, at age one, had just started to pull herself up to a standing position. Both my husband Ed and I were sitting right next to her and talking. Suddenly, Chantal reached up to a table that had previously been out of her reach and pulled a just-poured cup of hot coffee onto her face. Thanks to good luck and the miracle of ice water, our toddler was fine, but Ed and I have never forgotten this incident even after all these years.

The problem was that Ed and I were simply not prepared for the fact that our daughter could reach more from a standing position than she could when she was crawling on the floor. As soon as we understood, we moved things out of her way, watched her as best we could, and worked hard at teaching her to understand phrases like "*Hot!*" and "*Don't touch!*"

As parents, we can prevent many upsetting experiences by anticipating what is going to change when a child reaches a new level of development. Whether the issues are about People Safety or anything else, each change in skill, awareness, and situation leads to a need for reassessment. As children get older, we can expect changes in several areas.

Their abilities increase. This brings both more risks, as they have more freedom, and more opportunities to learn.

Their understanding increases. Children may worry about new situations or problems as they become more aware of them. As their understanding and knowledge of the world grows, our ability to discuss things with them also grows.

Their boundaries change. The preschooler who sat for hours on our laps and told us everything becomes a preteenager with a great need for privacy and personal space.

They go to more places and meet more people. Part of what makes life interesting and exciting is being able to do new things, but assuming that each new place and person will be okay or not okay is a mistake. Instead, our job as adults is to pay attention to potential problems and to give children tools both for telling us about their concerns and for finding solutions.

Their need for independence grows. We do not want to abandon children before they are ready, but we do want to support their development by fostering their independence and ability to care for themselves.

Over time, children will eventually grow *from* being in our arms, *to* holding our hands, *to* being within our reach, *to* staying where we can see and hear them, *to* being close enough to get back to us quickly, *to* being required to tell us what they are doing, *to* going somewhere without any supervision at all.

By being prepared for the results of the many changes that life brings, we can protect our children from most harm while teaching them how to protect themselves.

REPLACING DENIAL AND PANIC WITH AWARENESS AND CHOICES

When people are taken by surprise in an emergency like a natural disaster, a car accident, or an attack, their first feeling is likely to be one of denial. When faced with any unexpected situation, good or bad, it's normal to think, "I don't believe it! This can't be really happening!"

Disbelief can cause people to try to ignore a problem, making the situation more dangerous. A friend of mine told me this story: "My parents did not want to believe that the river near our farm was about to overflow – despite the pounding rain, the evidence of our own eyes, and the evacuations being strongly recommended by our fire department. Although I argued desperately, they insisted that our house would be fine because it had always been fine before. Unfortunately, the river did flood, suddenly making the road impassible. As our home filled with water and mud, we had to abandon all our possessions and wait on the roof to be rescued. We would have lost less and faced less trauma if they'd gotten out of denial sooner!"

Getting stuck for an instant in denial is normal, but we can train our children, and ourselves, to get unstuck quickly. The sooner we can get through our denial and pay attention, the sooner we can start taking appropriate action.

When people feel threatened by danger, fear triggers a flood of adrenaline. Often, this rush of adrenaline causes us to go on "automatic pilot." Think of a deer that stands frozen in the middle of the road and then suddenly dashes right into an oncoming car. Standing still and then zigzagging fast can help a deer escape from a mountain lion, but the same response creates a safety problem when the danger is an automobile. Like deer, people commonly panic when they are full of adrenaline. We often do not recognize potential problems or select our safest choices if we go on automatic pilot and start acting out of habit. Running away from a threat in a panic can make a situation more dangerous.

"My nephew and his friends were waiting for me to pick them up outside a big store in downtown San Francisco," one upset uncle said. "A gang of older teens drove up and threatened them. The boys panicked and ran in all directions. A couple of them were caught and beaten up. A car almost hit one because he ran into the street. If only they had kept their wits about them, they would have realized that the big, self-opening doors of the store were directly behind them. They could have stayed together, backed up, and gotten help inside the store."

Automatic behaviors can lead to many kinds of trouble if kids don't know when they can make a different choice. For example, most adults try to teach children to be kind, friendly, polite, and cooperative. But children need to know when *not* doing what they're told is a better choice.

"My six-year-old son, Chad, is a pleaser," Chad's mother said regretfully. "I've always told him to be a good boy, and his teacher has praised him for being so obedient. Yesterday, Chad suddenly had to go to the toilet urgently, but he listened quietly when his teacher told all the children to sit down and work. He eventually got so desperate that he couldn't talk at all and ended up wetting his pants.

"I feel awful that Chad was embarrassed, but I'm glad that nothing worse happened. We're going to be changing that 'always do what adults tell you' habit to a 'notice what you need and speak up to take care of yourself' habit!"

We don't have to beat ourselves up every time we learn a parenting life lesson like this one. We don't have to hold ourselves to perfect ideals – we need to have the courage to learn from our mistakes! As poet Maya Angelou says, "You did then what you knew how to do, and when you knew better you did better." This is true for us, and our children.

Life is always throwing out new challenges, especially for growing kids. Rehearsing solutions for different problems prepares children to make conscious decisions instead of getting stuck in denial or reacting without thinking. Kidpower training increases peoples' awareness so that they can avoid problems before they get serious. Our training also increases students' skills in dealing with dangerous or confusing situations. Having these skills helps people move past denial and panic, opening up more safe choices of how to respond in a variety of situations.

KIDPOWER'S UNDERLYING PRINCIPLE –
EASY TO AGREE WITH, HARD TO LIVE BY

Kidpower's Underlying Principle states: "The safety and self-esteem of a child are more important than *anyone's* embarrassment, inconvenience, or offense!"

This principle seems easy to agree with, but it can be hard to live by.

Right now, you might be thinking, "Well, *of course* I agree with this principle!" That's great, but try asking yourself these questions: Do I hate to be embarrassed? Do I try to avoid embarrassing others? Do I hate to be interrupted when I'm busy? Do I dislike bothering most other people? Do I get upset when other people get mad at me? Do I hate the feeling of being angry myself?

In my parent education workshops, when I ask these questions, most of the adults will say yes and agree that their children usually feel the same way. Most people don't like being bothered, embarrassed, or annoyed. And most people don't like having to embarrass, bother, or upset others. While most of us believe that safety and self-esteem are more important, these uncomfortable feelings are powerful social forces that can work against our upholding this belief.

Too many children have been harmed because their caregivers didn't teach them to put their safety first. Too often, these children did not want to do something embarrassing, like yell for help. Or, they didn't want to be rude to someone who was acting nice to them, even though that person was crossing their boundaries. Or, they didn't want to bother a busy adult when they had a safety problem.

When we are making hard decisions about what behaviors we are going to model and where to draw the line with other people, keeping Kidpower's underlying principle in mind can help us to make the best choices for our kids.

TEACHING PEOPLE SAFETY IN WAYS THAT BUILD CONFIDENCE, NOT FEAR

Many times, parents don't want to discuss personal safety issues with their children because they are afraid of damaging their children's trust in the world as a safe, happy place. Or, when something frightening happens in the news or in their community, some parents will try to make themselves feel safer by venting their fears to their children in a way that upsets their children without protecting them.

First of all, as adults, we need to separate our fears from our children's needs. We can discuss our worries with other caring adults, but our children do not need our anxiety. They need our faith that they can learn to protect themselves and our help in learning how.

If something bad happens, managing our children's information diet is every bit as important as managing their food diet. Hearing vivid details over and over and seeing the adults in their lives upset can be emotionally damaging for children. As parents, our job is to stay aware of what our children are hearing from adults, their friends, and the news – and to be careful about what we are saying when they can overhear us, even if they don't seem to be paying attention. In a calm, reassuring way, we can address any questions they might have about what they've heard, without providing upsetting details. Instead of focusing on the bad things that have happened, we can give them tools for keeping themselves safe most of the time.

For example, I think it is unfortunate that in English, *stranger* rhymes with *danger,* making it so easy to put those words together. Children are not served well by believing that the world is full of dangerous people they don't know. At Kidpower, we talk about "Stranger Safety" instead. We teach children that "most people are good" and that this means that most strangers are good. Rather than focusing on the bad things that sometimes happen, we encourage parents and caregivers to focus on teaching and practicing the specific skills and behaviors children can use to stay safe with strangers, as well as the rules and skills that will help them interact with people that they do know well.

LEARNING AND PRACTICING PEOPLE SAFETY SKILLS
TO BUILD INDEPENDENCE

Just talking about problems can cause children to become more worried without making them safer. However, successful practice in taking charge of their emotional and physical safety can increase children's competence and reduce their anxiety.

Instead of dwelling on the bad things that sometimes happen, parents can empower children by giving them opportunities to practice the following Kidpower skills in contexts that are relevant to their lives.

- Walking and acting with awareness, calm, and confidence

- Checking first with their adults before they change their plan about what they are doing, where they are going, and who they are with (including people they know)

- Checking first with their adults before they let a person or animal they don't know well get close to them (or thinking first if they don't have an adult to check with)

- Moving out of reach if something or someone might be unsafe

- Setting strong, respectful boundaries with people they know

- Protecting their feelings from hurtful words

- Staying in charge of what they say and do, in order to make their safest choices

- Making a safety plan for how to get help everywhere they go

- Taking charge of bullying in ways that helps them protect themselves and build stronger communities

- Being persistent in getting help from busy adults

• Understanding that the safety rules are different in emergencies where they cannot check first and need to get help

• Yelling and running to safety if they are scared

• Using self-defense skills to escape and get to safety if someone is being dangerous and they cannot leave and get help

In Kidpower workshops, we spend time role-playing these situations, and you can do this at home, too. (Our *Kidpower Safety Comics* are designed to guide parents through this process.) When you practice these skills together, lead with the same spirit you might use to help a child learn how to swim or ride a bike: keep your attitude upbeat and focus on supporting their success without turning your attention to the bad things that might happen if a child were to drown or be hit by a car.

If you feel yourself becoming anxious or upset when you are working with your child, take a break and practice again later. Children learn much better when their adults are calm. This is sometimes easier said than done when you are worried about your child's safety, but being able to practice together in a calm way is essential for your child's development of Kidpower personal safety skills.

For example, a common question parents ask is, "How can I teach my vulnerable young children to be careful of strangers without making them afraid of everyone?"

First of all, be sure that you are calm yourself when you talk to your children. If you sound anxious, they will pick up on that. Talking about "Stranger Danger" or focusing on scary stories can increase fear and anxiety for both of you. Instead, tell your children in a matter-of-fact way that you believe that most people are *good,* and that this means that most strangers are good, but that a few people have problems that might cause them to hurt kids.

Tell your children that they do *not* have to worry about strangers if they follow your safety rules – and there are rules that are specific to interacting with strangers. If young children are by themselves, the safety rule is to come and *check first* with you before they get close to or talk with anyone they don't know well. You can role-play this with your children. Pretend that a friendly-acting stranger is approaching your children, and have them practice coming to you to check first before talking to someone they don't know.

Discuss with your children specific examples about what it means to know someone well or not. For example, you might say, "The mail carrier is a very familiar person that you see almost every day, but this person is still a stranger. We don't know where the mail carrier lives or anything about her family. Your teacher was a stranger to you the first day of school, but it was okay for you to stay with him without me because I told you it was okay. Now that you've spent lots of time together, your teacher is not a stranger to you anymore." As you go about your daily lives, ask them to point out who is a stranger and who is not, and why.

When your children get old enough to be on their own without you, their safety rule is to *think first* before interacting with a stranger, check with you when necessary, and know how to *get help*. There are some situations in which kids can't check first and will need to decide on the best way to get help from a stranger. Discuss and practice different safety plans for getting help from strangers if your children cannot find you to check with first. For example, this could include a conversation about making a safety plan to follow if you ever get separated from each other in a large store. Then the child would want to ask for help from the person at the checkout counter, or if that doesn't work, a kid could seek out a woman with children and ask her to help look for you.

In our Kidpower workshops, we talk about other emergencies

when kids cannot check first. If a kid is legitimately experiencing an emergency himself, we want him to know that it is okay to get help from firefighters, paramedics, or a search party, even though these people are technically "strangers." On the other hand, if a stranger approaches a child with an emergency, the child should go find her grownups in charge and ask them to get help.

Remember that most of the people who harm children are not strangers, but people they know. For this reason, children need to know that, even with people they know, their safety plan is to check with their parents or other adults in charge before they change the original plan regarding whom they are with, where they are going, and what they are doing. At Kidpower, we tell a true story about a father who got off work early and picked up his son, who was walking home, to go get pizza. Unfortunately, they both forgot to tell the boy's mother, who tried calling her husband and, when she couldn't reach him, called the police! When the duo was finally found at the local pizza parlor, the mother was incredibly relieved, and understandably angry, too.

You can practice checking first before changing the plan by saying, "Let's imagine I'm a kid your age who lives next door. Suppose I'm trying to get you to come over and play." Pretend to be a kid inviting your child to come and do something fun. Coach your child to say, "I need to check first!" firmly and politely. Try to talk your child out of checking first by saying, "But your mom already knows. And it will take too long! Anyway, only babies have to ask their moms!" Coach your child to walk away from you, saying in a clear, confident voice, "I still need to check first!"

Children need to know how to set boundaries like the one above using persistent, respectful, and powerful words and actions, even when the other person is unhappy. Boundary-setting skills with people they know can protect children in case someone tries to do something harmful to them – and also can build better relationships. Since many adults find setting boundaries challenging, this can be an opportunity for the whole family to grow.

SETTING BOUNDARIES WITH PEOPLE YOU KNOW

Kidpower has four principles for setting personal boundaries with people you know:

We each belong to ourselves. This means not just our bodies, but also our time, our space, and our feelings.

Some things are not a choice. Other people have boundaries too, which we need to understand and respect. We need to follow the rules of our school or family as long as these rules are safe and everybody knows about them. For children, things to do with health and safety are usually not their choice.

Problems should not be secrets. Also, touch and games should not be a secret. Presents someone gives you or favors someone does for you should not be a secret.

Keep telling until you get help. If you have a problem, your job is to find an adult you trust and be persistent until you get the help you need. It is never too late to tell, and, if one adult does not help you, find another.

Real life is more complicated than any set of rules. This is why, in our Kidpower workshops, we coach children so that they are successful in rehearsing boundary-setting skills applying these principles through role-plays about situations that are relevant to their lives. We encourage parents to practice these skills at home with their children, and teachers to practice at school.

Studies have shown that just raising awareness about problems, without practicing skills to deal with them, can raise anxiety. Practicing skills to rehearse how to handle different situations almost always reduces anxiety and builds competence. Parents tend to feel more awkward about these rehearsals than kids! If you're nervous about role-playing, remember to capture the spirit of your children's imaginative play.

For example, you could say, "Use your imagination and pretend I'm a friend your age who wants to roughhouse, but you don't feel like it." Start acting like you want to wrestle and coach your child to step back, move your hands away, and say in a firm, polite voice, "Please stop. I don't want to wrestle." Act as if you have hurt feelings and coach your child to say, "I don't want to hurt your feelings. I just don't want to wrestle!"

PREPARING CHILDREN FOR MORE INDEPENDENCE

The process of preparing children for more independence includes the following steps, which build upon the foundation of Kidpower skills:

1) Making realistic assessments about your child in each situation

2) Learning and continuing to practice Kidpower skills as a family

3) Co-piloting with your child to field-test the use of skills in the real world

4) Conducting trial runs with adult backup to rehearse independence in controlled doses

5) Keeping communication open with listening, ongoing checking in, and review of skills

People Safety skills are described in the two previous sections, and the other steps are explained in the sections that follow.

MAKING REALISTIC ASSESSMENTS

Parents often ask Kidpower trainers some variation of the question, How will I know when my children are old enough to do something on their own? For example:

When can he play alone in the front yard?

Is she ready to walk to school by herself?

When can he stay overnight with friends?

Are they old enough to ride the city bus?

The answer is that it depends. There is no magic age when children are ready for certain activities. It depends on the specific situation and on the skills of the particular child.

For example, suppose your daughter wants to go to a friend's house for an overnight birthday party. Assessment questions about the situation might include: How well do I know this friend's parents? If I don't know them well, can I arrange to meet them and make sure that I feel comfortable letting my daughter go? What activities are planned? What level of supervision will be provided? Who else will be at home?

Assessment questions about your daughter's skills include: Does my daughter know what our safety rules are and how to follow them? Can she speak up if she feels uncomfortable? Can she say no to her friends if they start to do something unsafe even if she feels embarrassed? Does she know how to call me anytime, even in the middle of the night, if she needs help?

Suppose your son wants to walk to school by himself. Assessment questions about the situation might include: What is the route to school like? What hazards are along the way? What is the traffic like? Are there crossing guards, cross walks, and stoplights? Are there interesting, but potentially dangerous, things that might tempt my son into changing his plan, such as ponds, animals, or construction? What kinds of people, such as strangers, gangs, or bullies, might cause a safety problem for him? Are there stores, neighbors, or other places he could get help if he needs to?

Assessment questions about your son's skills include: How aware and careful is my son? Does he get lost in daydreaming, or can he pay attention to the traffic and people around him? Does my son understand and know how to follow our safety rules? Can he remember to check with me first before he changes his plan even if something looks very interesting or his friends start pressuring him? If someone challenges him in a rude way, can my son walk away from trouble and get help, or will he feel the need to prove himself? Can he interrupt a busy adult to get help if he needs to? Can my son run, yell, and get help if he's scared?

By making realistic assessments, we can determine whether a specific child is ready to handle a specific situation independently and, if not, what this child would need to know and be able to do in order to become ready. We need to remember that children develop skills at different paces and have different personalities. What is safe for one child at a given age in a given situation might take longer or require extra precautions to be safe for another child.

If you are unsure or concerned that your child might not make the safest choice, or if you feel that your child isn't ready to do something independently, take the time to review skills with him or her or make different plans that provide more supervision and support.

CO-PILOTING TO FIELD-TEST SKILLS IN THE REAL WORLD

Once children have been successful in practicing People Safety skills through role-plays, the next challenge is for them to learn how to generalize the use of these skills to different kinds of real-life situations. Co-piloting is a technique that can be very effective in helping you see how well your child can stay safe out in the real world. This is how co-piloting works: before you let your child do an activity alone, you tag along on that activity with your child, letting your child lead the way. This gives your child the opportunity to show you what he or she can do, and it gives you the opportunity to notice any unexpected problems and to ask questions to check on your child's understanding.

For example, when Chantal was five, she wanted to be able to walk across the street from her summer school program to her brother's day care without having me come and get her. Even though the school was directly across the street from the day care, there were lots of parents around, and the street had a crossing guard, I was very nervous about the idea. I followed Chantal as she walked ahead of me on the route she would take from her summer school door to the day care center, so that I could see exactly what she was doing.

As we walked, I peppered her with questions: "If someone stops their car and starts to talk with you, what will you do? If someone has a puppy, what will you do? If someone you know tries to give you a ride, what will you do?" My child's calm awareness as she walked, the level of supervision around, and her answers reassured me that she was ready to take this step toward independence. However, while co-piloting, we noticed one glitch – the day care center door was sometimes locked. Co-piloting made it possible to see this problem ahead of time and make a plan for the day care staff to watch for Chantal, and for how, if need be, she could find someone to let her inside.

Another idea on the use of co-piloting came from one of our most experienced instructors, Erika Leonard, when she was teaching a workshop on Internet safety. Since many children are ahead of their parents when it comes to use of the Internet and other technologies, parents often feel unsure about how to set boundaries for and keep track of their children's digital activities.

Erika suggests that parents and their children co-pilot these activities together, exploring new technologies side by side. This way, parents can discuss with their children how the safety rules apply to each particular situation. Linda Criddle's chapter, "How to Say *Yes* to Your Kids' Online Activities," explores this issue in greater detail.

CONDUCTING TRIAL RUNS WITH ADULT BACKUP TO DEVELOP CHILDREN'S INDEPENDENCE

Rather than giving blanket permission for activities requiring more independence, we can let children develop their skills and understanding by having trial runs with our backup. That way, they have the opportunity to do things on their own while having easy access to adult support in case they need help.

For example, my friend Marsha's young teenagers wanted to camp with their friends without adult supervision. They had had lots of experience camping, but never by themselves. Marsha took a campsite in the next loop from theirs so that she could be accessible just in case they needed her. Her children found out that camping on their own was a lot of fun – and a lot of work!

KEEPING THE LINES OF COMMUNICATION OPEN

Children are safest when they know that the adults in their lives are paying attention to what they are doing and are helpful people to come to with problems. Even after children are used to doing an activity on their own, it is important to continue to check in and review safety plans and skills. People can change. Situations can change. Problems can develop that were not there before.

One girl tearfully told me in a workshop about her best friend, whose parents were going through a divorce. Her own parents just assumed that she was still happy spending the night at her friend's house, since she had done so for years. Unfortunately, there was lots of drinking and fighting going on in this home now, and this girl felt afraid for herself and her friend. We made a plan for how she could talk with her parents and get their help, perhaps arranging for her friend to stay at their house rather than trading back and forth.

Remind children that problems should not be secrets and that you want to know what's happening in their lives. Be a helpful adult to come to by listening without judgment or lecturing.

Once in a while, ask your children, "Is there anything you've been wondering or worrying about that you haven't told me?" If you listen with calm appreciation to their answers, you help your children develop the habit of telling you how things are going for them so that you can continue to support them in taking charge of their emotional and physical safety.

BEING REEDUCATED BY THE NEXT GENERATION

I want to conclude by saying that finding the balance between independence and safety is not an easy process. As the lucky grandmother of a toddler, I am being reeducated about the challenges of raising a child – the overwhelming love and heart-stopping vulnerability I remember from when my own children were young are again part of my daily reality. Once again, I see the world with new eyes. My granddaughter's passionate drive for independence often conflicts with my intense determination to keep her safe. Sometimes I hold on too tightly. Sometimes I let go too quickly. I have to remind myself of the Kidpower sayings, "Mistakes are part of learning" and "You don't have to be perfect to be great!" As parents, remember that there is no greater gift you can give your children than to be joyful about who they are as you give them the tools to grow into who they will become.

How to Say "Yes" to Your Kids' Online Activities

Linda Criddle

Linda Criddle is a 13-year Microsoft veteran and internationally recognized leader in Internet safety and technology. She is President of LOOK**BOTH**WAYS Inc., which develops cutting-edge safety software and provides consultation to the online industry, governments, law enforcement, and educators. Linda is also President of the LOOK**BOTH**WAYS Foundation, a non-profit organization dedicated to bringing Internet curriculum to schools and educational materials to consumers of all ages. Linda is the author of *Look Both Ways: Help Protect Your Family on the Internet* and *Using the Internet Safely for Seniors for Dummies.* Linda also serves as the President of the Safe Internet Alliance, an advocacy group dedicated to bringing a safer online experience to all consumers. For more information about Internet safety or to contact Linda, go to www.iLookBothWays.com.

Mention the words *Internet* and *child* in the same sentence and most parents start getting anxious – and it's no wonder, given the sensationalized press coverage of many online crimes.

Fortunately, reality is far gentler most of the time. With some basic safety principles, skills, and choices, you and your children can confidently explore the web, try new services, and be safer. This chapter covers how you can feel confident about saying yes when your kids ask to use new online services, and how you can make online safety a positive, collaborative process.

You already know how to spot and avoid many risks in your physical environment, and these safety skills have become so ingrained that you often automatically use them throughout your day without even thinking about it. For example, you learned long ago to manage situations like crossing the street and no longer consciously tell yourself: *look both ways, stop, look, and listen,* or *only cross on green.* Because you easily learned the traffic rules, you are confident when teaching your child and confident that your child can master the same skills.

Just as you do in everyday life, you can spot and avoid risks in your online environment. If you have not yet learned online safety skills, they can seem overwhelming, and you may be fearful of helping your kids navigate the Internet successfully. *Don't panic.* Being safer online does not require you to be a "techspert" or know how to develop software. By the end of this chapter, you will understand how making safe choices online can become an automatic reflex, and you will have more confidence in your ability to help your children master the skills they need for a safer, more positive online experience.

WHAT IS A PREDATOR?

When people hear the phrase *online predator,* they immediately assume the discussion is about pedophiles. This is not accurate. The term *predator* includes anyone that preys on and abuses another.

The term *predator* is broader than the term *criminal,* as *not all forms of abuse are criminalized, but all forms of abuse are predatory.*

What all predators have in common is that they choose to abuse others by exploiting weaknesses and preying on vulnerabilities.

Abuse falls into four categories:

Emotional abuse includes cyberbullying, harassment, and preying on peoples' emotions to commit cons and scams

Financial abuse includes financial scams, ID theft, and fraudulent e-commerce sites

Physical abuse includes all forms of bodily harm as well as theft of possessions from private property, such as homes, businesses, or cars

Reputational abuse includes damaging or assuming another's reputation

WHAT ARE THE KEY FACTORS THAT PUT INTERNET USERS AT RISK?

Many adults think that there are three primary risks for kids online – sexual predators, inappropriate material, and cyberbullies. However, this view fails to account for the underlying factors that put users at risk of online abuse. Users of any age expose themselves to Internet risk when they:

Fail to consider what information they actually share, its value, and whether they should share it at all

Fail to identify trustworthiness or lack of trustworthiness in the people, Web sites, content, and businesses they interact with

Fail to understand predatory behavior and motives in the broadest sense, including bullying, stalking, scamming, thieving, and sexual predation

Once you understand these core risk factors, you can minimize them for yourself and your children by assessing how these may apply to any new online activity or service you or your kids want to start using. But the time to do this is *in advance* of participating in any new online activity or service.

HOW INTERNET RISKS OCCUR

Knowing what risks are common to all users is the first step in developing safety consciousness. Understanding *how* these risks are manifested and what you can do to reduce or eliminate them is the next step.

A basic understanding of how Internet risks occur helps to place any Internet safety advice in context. Take a moment to consider each of the five factors that contribute to the current online environment.

    Lack of knowledge about tools and services
    + Carelessness in actions taken
    + Unintentional (or intentional) exposure by others
    + Flaws and gaps in technology
    + Holes in consumer protection standards
    _____
    = Deliberate criminal acts

Lack of knowledge. Consumers of every age and level of technical expertise lack broad online safety education. First, you need to learn how to use online products and services, but this alone is not enough.

You must also have a basic understanding of how predators may use the tools so you can act defensively – just as you learn to act defensively when driving a car or walking down the street.

Carelessness. Even when we "know better," we make mistakes. Usually those mistakes occur when we're tired, rushed, or don't have a complete understanding of the risks involved. In the tangible world, carelessness frequently results in pain. You put your hand on a hot stove, and you get immediate feedback telling you that it was a poor choice; you work too quickly in the kitchen with a knife, and your nicked finger warns you to exercise more caution. Unfortunately, on the Internet, there is rarely an immediate or obvious cause and effect between an action and its consequence.

This lack of immediate feedback means many victims of online abuse don't recognize that it was an action they (or someone else) took online that made them vulnerable to predation. Burglars don't leave little cards saying, "Hey, thanks for letting me know you were going out of town." Bullies don't mention that they read on your blog about your fight with your friends, so they know you don't have anyone to stick up for you. And scammers certainly don't say, "I thought I'd get to know you because you sure sound like a sucker for financial fraud."

Unintentional exposure by other people or devices. The information or action that puts you or your child at risk may not be something you, or they, posted. It may be something a teacher, a school, another parent, a grandparent, a friend, the government, or an after-school program placed on a publicly accessible Internet site that exposed you or your child. It is quite likely that *information from a number of sources* was combined to create the risk.

Alternatively, your home computer (or mobile phone or other connected device) may not be fully protected by security software and strong passwords, and may allow sensitive information to be compromised.

Or, perhaps the information is exposed when a company's database, friend's computer, or cell phone, with an address book, saved photos, and access to social network accounts, is lost or stolen.

Technology flaws. Not all online services are equally safe. In the same way different car companies vary on their safety records, Internet products and services may be more or less safe. Online products and services can put consumers at risk – either because the companies who offer them fail to secure their customers' data and are hacked, or because they fail to build adequate safeguards and safety messaging into their products.

It would be great if consumers could consult a comprehensive list that ranked each company or service on safety features, privacy settings, and consumer-friendly policies, but this doesn't yet exist. You can, however, ask around and compare alternatives. For example, you have probably heard about the social networking sites Facebook and MySpace, but there are many other similar sites that take considerably stronger approaches to safety and user privacy – as well as sites that do a poorer job.

At the end of this chapter you will find an *Internet Safety Bill of Rights* to help you consider what expectations you should have, and what you should demand, of online services.

Holes in consumer protection standards. The products and services we use in our day-to-day lives undergo rigorous safety testing. Everything from the food we eat to the cars we drive must meet safety standards. Companies that fail to meet these standards are subject to product recall notices, fines, and lawsuits.

This assumption of safety cannot be extended to the online environment, because there are no compliance standards in place. Though segments of Internet industries have best practices, these are not required standards, and there is no established entity that oversees consumer safety online. This lack of oversight means it is critical for you to check the reputation of the companies and Web sites you, or your children, want to use and understand that your best interests are not inherently protected.

Criminal and abusive acts. Placing the word *cyber* in front of

-criminal, -thief, -robber, -molester, -bully, -scammer, or *-predator* only changes the criminal's tools, not their motivations or goals. They still want to destroy your reputation, dominate or abuse you, or steal your money.

Criminals and abusers have always exploited gaps in laws, naïve consumers, flaws in prevention tools, and careless actions in any environment. What makes the online world particularly attractive to all types of predators is that many people are less prepared to defend themselves against online exploitation. This is true of any newly adopted technology – it happened with the telephone and the fax machine, and it will happen again when the next "new thing" comes along.

However, you can be as safe in the online world as you are in your everyday life.

CREATING AN ENVIRONMENT
FOR FAMILY SAFETY COLLABORATION

To create a collaborative environment for online safety, you need three things: respect, understanding, and a shared sense of safety.

Don't set out to control your kids when the goal is to create a safe, respectful environment. Understanding the limitations of monitoring tools – which can be great for very young kids but is almost completely ineffective with teens – opens the way to a more collaborative approach to Internet safety that begins with a family conversation.

When speaking with your children, avoid the term *Parental Controls*. It inherently creates antagonism where none is needed – nobody wants to be controlled, least of all youth trying to find their own identities and gain a measure of independence. The term does not represent what you want to achieve, which is to help your children stay safer online and protect the entire family.

Parental control also incorrectly implies it is only youth who may be placing the family at risk in their online actions.

> Internet safety isn't something you can effectively impose on anyone over the age of ten – if they don't buy-in to safety, they will find a way around any boundary you set.

Instead of antagonizing and patronizing youth by relying on spying, recording, and tattling on even their safest online conversations and legitimate activities, capitalize on the reality that people of all ages have a basic sense of self-preservation and are interested in their own safety most of the time. Your kids don't want to be bullied, stalked, scammed, disrespected, or have their identity stolen any more than you do. Additionally, your kids don't want to expose you or their siblings, friends, or grandparents to abuse – whether it's burglary, identity theft, financial fraud, or physical harm.

Finding the best balance between supervision and independence for youth isn't easy, because there is no one-size-fits-all answer. But, how you choose to approach supervision and safety discussions will play a critical role in whether or not your children buy-in to your safety plan, and whether it helps build or erode trust between you.

Start out the conversation by identifying what it takes for each member of the family to feel safe. What information are they comfortable sharing and what do they want to keep private? Discuss how an action taken by one family member impacts the safety of other family members. For example:

> If a parent chooses to place their full name, city and state, and the names of their children on their public profile, then everyone in the family has this information exposed

If a family member places information publicly saying the
family is going away on vacation, then the family's home
is at risk for burglary

Talk about how family respect means that everyone's need for
privacy and safety are respected. This respect requirement extends
to everyone's friends and acquaintances as well. Friends should
not "out" your family, and you should not "out" them or their
family online.

APPLYING THE "YES" PRINCIPLE

You now have the framework for discussing and implementing
safety in your own and your children's online experience. But
what safety precautions does it take to let your child use a *specific*
Internet service? The answer is to break down the service into its
component pieces: does it need a password or user name, does it
ask for location or photos, etc.? For each component, your child
needs both an awareness of the risks involved and a mastery of
the tangible skills required to protect them from those risks. As an
example, let's look at the component concepts, skills, and responsibilities required for younger and older children to use email.

Email Skills for Younger Kids

Your child asks to have an email account so they can talk to
Grandma and a few friends. You say, "Yes, of course you can use
email; we just need to be sure you understand the safety principles
and have the skills to use email safely."

Next, break down the features of your particular email service to
identify the skills and safety principles your child will need to understand and master. In this scenario for a young child, you will probably want to limit their interactions to people you trust and know.

∾

Concept: Safe email aliases (the part of the email address before the @ symbol).

Demonstrable Skill: Your child creates a safe email alias.

For children, aliases should not include their name, age, or location; also, aliases should not reference emotions or anything provocative. Make them fun, and take the time to help them make several choices that show they have mastered the skill.

Examples of poor choices include:

- suzie14Seattle@emailservice.com – shows first name, gender, age, and location

- JeffreySmith@emailservice.com – gives a full name (which may be appropriate for adults, but should never be exposed with children) which, when combined with any location information, makes a home address easy to obtain

- SexySantoros@emailservice.com – sexually suggestive and contains last name

Examples of good choices include:

- Fishfan@emailservice.com

- Soccerplayer@emailservice.com

- Stargazer@emailservice.com

Child's Responsibility: I will protect my email alias and not give it to strangers.

∽

Concept: Safe passwords.

Demonstrable Skill: Your child consistently creates strong passwords that include numbers, letters, and symbols.

Passwords do not have to be hard to remember – just hard to

guess. They should not include your child's name, age, or location, dates, family members' information, or anything else easily guessed. They should be at least eight characters in length and include a mix of letters, numbers, and symbols. Make creating strong passwords fun. Hint: text message shortcuts can make creating strong passwords easy.

- 2bOrNot2b? (to be or not to be, that is the question)
- ROFL@MyCat (rolling on the floor laughing at my cat)
- i8myCookie (I ate my cookie)
- I'mAGr8guy (I'm a great guy)

Take time to play with password options until your child has mastered the skill.

Child's Responsibility: I will not share my passwords with others, and I will not ask others to share their passwords with me; friends don't ask friends for passwords.

∾

Concept: Inappropriate content.

Demonstrable Skill: Your child notifies you when they suspect that content is inappropriate.

If your child is only emailing with people you know and trust, there should be little risk of inappropriate content sharing, but it can happen, and the time to talk about it is *before* an incident occurs. With younger kids, role-play how they can get your help, and with older kids, discuss the issue more deeply.

Child's Responsibility: If anything upsets me or feels wrong, I will talk to my parent about it.

The parent's responsibility is to respond appropriately – punishing your child by taking away their Internet access or freaking out will only mean they do not come to you next time there is a problem.

∾

Concept: Links and advertisements.

Demonstrable Skill: Your child correctly identifies and refrains from clicking on links and advertisements.

Again, if you have your child's email account set to only accept email from trusted contacts, you should have no trouble with spam, links, and advertisements. However, the time to teach is now, *before* an incident occurs. Friends may forward chain letters or include links to sites that unknowingly download malware or contain inappropriate advertisements. Even five-year-olds can easily understand that ads don't necessarily tell the truth and that they should not click on them. Show your child some flashy advertisements and help them see how these can be harmful and deceptive.

Child's Responsibility: I will not click on advertisements or links in emails without my parent's permission or help. I will not forward chain emails.

Email Skills for Older Kids

In this scenario, your child has been using a protected email account for a while and now wants to be able to send and receive email from people not on your secure list. You answer, "Yes, of course you can use email more broadly; we just need to be sure you understand the safety principles and have the skills to use the broader email functionality safely." Review the basic email skills and responsibilities above, and then make sure your child also understands and masters the following concepts.

Concept: Spam, scams, phishing attacks, and malware.

Demonstrable Skill: Your child consistently identifies spam email.

No matter how well you help your kids set their filters, some junk mail is going to get through, so they have to master the skill of identifying spam, scams, and phishing emails. Fortunately, it's easy to learn to spot these kinds of messages. Together, go to my Web site, www.iLookBothWays.com, and practice using the fun *Spot the Spam* skill-building series. Using these samples, you and your child will soon become experts at spotting and avoiding spam, scams, and phishing in email. Discuss with your child that no company is going to give them money, and that anyone who claims to be notifying them that they won the lottery, or has money to send to them, is lying. Discuss that attachments in email may contain malicious code – even if the sender is someone they know and trust. Before downloading something they do not absolutely trust, they should seek your help.

Child's Responsibility: I will protect myself and my family from phishing, scams, and malicious software. If anything upsets me or feels wrong, I will talk to my parents about it.

As with identifying inappropriate content, this skill carries a responsibility for parents to respond to problems appropriately. Punishing your child by taking away their Internet access or freaking out will only mean they do not come to you next time there is a problem.

∾

Concept: Email claims are not inherently true.

Demonstrable Skill: Your child uses online resources to verify the validity of email claims.

In addition to learning *Spot the Spam* skills, there are several sites, like www.snopes.com, where you can look up to see if the email is a known scam. Go to Snopes and let your child use the site until they have mastered searching the site for answers.

Child's Responsibility: I will take the time to find out if an email is telling me the truth before acting on it or forwarding it.

∾

Concept: Report abuse.

Demonstrable Skill: Your child appropriately reports several types of email abuse.

There are several forms of email abuse, and reporting these requires different actions. If the email is spam, phishing, or a scam, teach your child to use the JUNK button in your email program to delete and report it in one step. If the email is from someone who is being mean or hurtful – cyberbullying – teach them to report it to the service using the service's REPORT ABUSE button. If the company does not clearly display a report abuse button, teach them to contact the company's customer support team and to come to you for more help. If the security violation is that your child's email account has been taken over by someone else, teach them how to contact the service and get their account reset.

Child's Responsibility: I will report abuse because doing so protects me, my family, and the online community. I will report cyberbullying because no one has the right to threaten, intimidate, or humiliate me. The cyberbully bears full responsibility for their actions, and I will not retaliate by cyberbullying them back. I will not tell anyone my password, and if my password is compromised, I will get help to fix it immediately.

∾

Concept: Stop chain email.

Demonstrable Skill: Your child identifies chain email and deletes it.

A particularly frustrating email phenomenon is the virtual chain letter. These messages may or may not contain malicious links or downloads, but they always clog up email servers and jeopardize the continuous flow of legitimate email. Teach your child how to identify chain email and to always delete it.

Child's Responsibility: I understand that forwarding chain emails harms the overall flow of legitimate email across servers, and can spread malicious content and expose my own and my friends' email accounts to scammers. I will not forward chain email.

❧

Concept: Respect others' privacy when forwarding email.
Demonstrable Skill: Your child consistently uses the BCC: line when forwarding email to more than one person.

Protecting the privacy of others is a very critical Internet safety skill. Teach your child how to use the BCC: (blind carbon copy) line provided by your email service. Teach them to never send an email that exposes their friends' email aliases to others. If they want to send an email to people who do not know each other, they should place everyone's email on the BCC: line and only place their own email alias on the TO: line.
Child's Responsibility: I will not expose my friends' or family's email accounts to others without their permission. I will use the BCC: line to protect peoples' identities.

❧

Concept: Respect others' privacy even when you are no longer friends.
Demonstrable Skill: You child continues to protect the privacy of former friends.

Kids' – and adults' – alliances change: best friends have falling outs, a boyfriend one day may be an enemy the next, and so on. However, something told in confidence during friendship should remain in confidence even if your child and the other child are no longer friends. Teach your child integrity both offline and online. It's not just a critical Internet skill; it's a critical life skill.
Child's Responsibility: I will respect the privacy of others even if I no longer like them.

❧

Concept: Terms and conditions of use and account settings.

Demonstrable Skills: Your child understands and selects their account settings to reflect their privacy boundaries; your child reads and either declines or agrees to a service's terms and conditions of use.

All email services have privacy and safety boundaries and terms and conditions for use. Before kids take on the ownership of their own email account, they need to know what settings are available and how to use them. Walk them through the safety and privacy settings of the email service they want to use. Explain to them what the settings do and discuss what settings are appropriate. Depending on the age of your child, it may be appropriate to set these boundaries unilaterally, or to negotiate the boundaries based on your child's mastery of skills and willingness to accept social responsibility and consequences. Help your child establish their settings and make it clear that you will revisit their settings periodically to be sure that they are still a good fit as they grow in age and experience.

Before kids take on the ownership of their email account, they also have to understand and agree to abide by the service's terms and conditions. In some cases they may find that they don't like a site's terms and choose to use another site that is perhaps more respectful of their right to privacy. This is a good lesson in and of itself.

Child's Responsibility: I understand that by taking on the responsibility for my own email account, I am responsible for selecting account settings that protect my privacy and safety and the privacy and safety of my family. I understand that using an Internet service requires that I follow the terms and conditions the site sets for users. I have read the site's terms and agree to follow their requirements.

∾

By breaking it down into elements, you can easily see how to master – and teach – Internet safety as it relates to email. Once your child has demonstrated to you that they have mastered these concepts, skills, and responsibilities, you can confidently say, "Yes, you are now ready, and you have my permission, to use email."

It is important to note that mastery of these skills and acceptance of online social responsibilities are not just requirements for kids; they apply to users of all ages. Parents frequently expose more information about themselves and others than their children do and are more at risk for spam scams.

It is critical to understand, and to help your child understand, that the responsibility for demonstrating mastery of the concepts, skills, and responsibilities *lies with your child*. They need to be the one to take ownership of their online actions and must be able to demonstrate to you their preparedness. Your responsibility is to help them learn. It's like swimming: until your child can demonstrate that they are able to safely swim across the pool, climb out, and follow the rules, they can't swim alone. The only one who can demonstrate this is the child herself.

There will be slip-ups, particularly when your child is first learning new skills or starting out on new online services. When mistakes happen, it is essential that you understand whether they erred because they did not clearly understand a safety concept, have not entirely mastered the skills needed, or willfully placed themselves or others in harm's way by shirking the responsibilities they have to themselves, their family, and the Internet community at large.

If the slip-up was caused by a lack of understanding or lack of skill mastery, the solution is to step back and review the concepts and skills and let your child practice these in a safe environment until they can again demonstrate their preparedness.

If the slip-up was deliberate, they have broken your trust and will need to figure out how to fix the mess and regain your trust *before* they regain the privilege of using that particular service or functionality. Again, it is your child's responsibility to show they are able to act appropriately. It is in their power to show they are up to the task, or not. This way, the blame doesn't land on you and some indefinable, arbitrary reason why you will or won't let them use an online service.

As your children step up to more advanced Internet services like social networking, the same steps apply. Break down the service to the features it offers and map out the concepts, skills, and responsibilities that accompany them. You can learn more about what is needed for several types of services on www.iLookBothWays.com.

You can, and should, say yes to your child's Internet use as soon as they have shown that they understand the concepts, accept the responsibilities, and have the skills needed to stay safe online.

As parents, our responsibility is to ensure that when our children reach the age of 18 and are ready to step out into the broader world, they are prepared to do so. Part of their preparation is the opportunity to learn and use all types of online tools and services. And as is true with other skills we teach our children, they need the opportunity to practice and sometimes fail in an environment where we are there to pick them up and help them get back on track.

Failing to prepare our children for our digital society is failing to prepare them for adult life. By breaking down each new online service into a concrete set of concepts, skills, and responsibilities, you can confidently help your children learn to use online tools safely – you can say *yes*.

A FINAL WORD ABOUT YOUR POWER
AND YOUR RIGHTS AS AN ONLINE CITIZEN

As you evaluate the services that you and your children use, understand the tremendous power you have as a consumer. If consumers are unhappy with a service and stop using it, the service will quite literally collapse. Let services know what you like and don't like, and encourage your friends and family to do the same.

As consumers you can – and should – vote with your feet if the experience you're having on a service doesn't meet your expectations. You can make a difference. Your safety rights won't be established in Internet programs and services overnight. But if you let companies know what you think, these rights will surely be delivered faster.

Your Internet Safety Bill of Rights

All Internet users have the right to a safe Internet experience. Your safety and the safety of your family on the Internet should not be left to afterthought features ("add-ons") or those requiring extra payment. You can't buy a new car without safety belts or air bags; you shouldn't have to settle for Internet products or services that fail to offer safety in the same basic way.

In a nutshell, I believe every online consumer has these rights:

1) You have the right to an informed online experience.

- You should know in advance about any potential risks of using Internet services such as social networks, dating sites, or instant message programs so you can make safe choices.

- You have the right to complete information about every safety feature in a product or service, and safety recommendations by feature should be easy to discover. At the bare minimum, you should be able to find safety information in the HELP section. Ideally, however, the program should give safety advice at relevant points, such as when you create a password, choose your privacy settings, or post a photo.

- When services are upgraded, you have the right to be informed in advance of new features or changes to existing features and their impact on your safety. Additionally, you should have a clear way to opt-out of any features you're uncomfortable with.

2) *You have the right to set your own terms for your online experience (within the constraints of the law).*

- You have the right to get content that matches your values and block content you do not wish to see, no matter what your age.

- You have the right to set boundaries so that you are only exposed to the level of potential risk you're comfortable with, whether you're more or less risk-averse. This includes being able to manage the online experience of minors in your care.

- You have the right to know if you are being monitored online and how you are being monitored: this includes which of your activities are being tracked and to whom they are being reported. Your children have this right, too.

3) *You have the right to expect online products and services to guard your safety and privacy.*

- You have the right to feel confident that products and services will not be released to the public without undergoing rigorous safety, privacy, and legal reviews and testing.

- You have the right to know the privacy and safety policies of online products and services. These should be easy to find and written in terms that are easy to understand.

- You have the right to easily report abuse of or through the products you and your family use. You also have the right to know how well the company enforces its policies and to expect immediate action from the company.

- You have the right to expect a product recall notice or alert if a significant safety risk is discovered in an online product or service.

For more information on Internet safety, visit Linda Criddle's Web site at www.iLookBothWays.com and search by topic or keyword. If you cannot find the answers to your questions within the site, you can use the AskLinda feature to get a personalized response.

section four

Finding Your Voice and Raising It for the Community

In our final section, we make the connection between individual action and the larger community. One of my biggest lessons as a new mother was that no matter how capable and competent I could possibly be, I was not going to be able to "do it all" on my own. I *needed* friends, family, and community. In what follows, we hear from four writers, backed by an online chorus, about the power of community to support and inspire us all.

Journalist and *PunditMom* blog author Joanne Bamberger explores her process of finding her political voice and becoming willing to use it. She had been political all her life, but it was only after becoming a mother to a daughter that she realized how critical it was to fight for the causes she believed in, for herself and all our kids. In "Becoming a Political Parent: PunditMom on Mothers Raising Their Voices Online," she encourages other parents to claim their political ideas and identities, find support, and share their perspectives with the world.

When thousands or millions of people combine their efforts and resources to work for common goals, real change can happen, as grassroots organizer Kristin Rowe-Finkbeiner reports in "Building a Family-friendly America: Challenge and Progress Through the Eyes of MomsRising.org." Since its inception in 2006, MomsRising.org, which works both online and in the real world, has grown to over one million members. MomsRising has been instrumental in passing paid parental leave in Washington State and New Jersey, and Kristin was invited to the White House to represent MomsRising at President Obama's bill signing of the *Lilly Ledbetter Fair Pay Act of 2009*.

Our final chapter, "It Takes a Motherhood," takes us full circle from our first chapter on self-care to discuss self-care in the context of community-care. Cooper Munroe and Emily McKhann, founders of TheMotherhood.com, discuss what their online community has meant to them and their members, and we hear from the members themselves. Cooper and Emily include dialogue from an online conversation they led (which involved both anthology contributors and TheMotherhood members) that discussed what being a courageous parent means to different people. The chat was a wonderful experience. It allowed us to take the concept of this anthology – initially a collaboration among the 13 contributors and myself – and open it up to a larger community. Everyone has something important to say, and TheMotherhood is an excellent example of how vital it is to have a community to share ideas with and allies to provide support when we need it.

Becoming a Political Parent: PunditMom on Mothers Raising Their Voices Online

Joanne Bamberger

Joanne Bamberger is a recovering attorney, journalist, politically progressive mom, and political analyst living in the shadow of the nation's capital. Known around the blogosphere as "Pundit-Mom," in addition to writing her own op-ed commentary blog, Joanne is a regular contributor to many news outlets, including *The Huffington Post* and *MOMocrats.* She is a former Contributing Editor at *BlogHer,* and a member of the inaugural class of the Progressive Women's Voices program at the Women's Media Center. Joanne's book, *Mothers of Intention,* based on her blog feature of the same name, will be published in the fall of 2010. Catch up with Joanne at www.PunditMom.com.

I've been a political geek all my life. I'm not really sure what gave me the bug, but whatever it was, I've had it for a long time. However, my journey through motherhood refined and amplified my true political voice, even though there have been times when it would have been easier to keep my beliefs to myself. I've found that other women say they have also felt more politically motivated after they had children, though when asked if they view themselves as political creatures, the answer is often a resounding no.

Growing numbers of mothers are awakening their political selves and embracing a model of civil discourse that moves away from the shouting matches that typify political debate in the mainstream media. My journey to political motherhood has been one of finding the courage to say and write what I believe, hoping that speaking up will help bring about the change I want to see for my daughter and stepdaughters.

Looking back, maybe it was the subscription to *Time* magazine my aunt and uncle gave me for Christmas when I was in middle school that created that first spark of political engagement, or maybe it was our cute high school civics teacher! It could have been the televised Watergate hearings I was glued to during the summer of 1974, even though my mother implored me to get some fresh air. Or it could have been the mock presidential convention I attended at our local college during my senior year in high school, where I proudly and nervously cast our delegation's "votes."

To the dismay of my über-practical parents, I majored in political science in college. Since it was the 1970s, I was more than familiar with the work of women's movement icons like Gloria Steinem, super-feminist and one of the founders of *Ms. Magazine*, and Betty Friedan, author of *The Feminine Mystique* and one of the founders of the National Organization for Women (NOW). But it was hard to get my teenage head around other notions that stood in opposition to my own worldview.

I'll never forget my naïve shock at the realization that there were others at the total opposite end of the women's political spectrum: women like Phyllis Schlafly, who organized the movement that single-handedly prevented the passage of the Equal Rights

Amendment, and Marabel Morgan, author of *The Total Woman*, a book dedicated to the art of pleasing your husband, complete with tips about greeting him at the door wearing nothing but Saran Wrap!

Even with many people working against the Equal Rights Amendment and for maintaining women's "traditional" roles, I was confident, in the way that only someone with very limited life experience can be, that I would be one of that lucky generation of women who would reap the benefits of Gloria and Betty's work, and not have to worry in my professional life about things like unequal pay, being passed over for promotion in favor of less-qualified men, or not being offered a chance to do something simply because of my second X chromosome.

While I couldn't get enough of the process, policy, and philosophy of politics, and even though I was totally excited by my political education and exposure to new ideas as a college student, I hadn't found my own political voice. I was still figuring out where I fit into the political landscape. I thought, *Who really cares what one farm girl from Pennsylvania thinks, and what difference would it make if I tell anyone?* A few other girls in my political science classes were also pretty reluctant to bring their voices to the table. Later, as a young journalist, I used the convenient excuse that since I covered politics for local radio and television stations, it was inappropriate to be outspoken about my own views because people would question my objectivity as a reporter.

As I moved through life and became more secure in my inner political geek and my ability to articulate my opinions, I still only shared my views with close friends and family. *Why rock the boat? Why create a debate where there didn't need to be one?* I reasoned. Despite having become a litigator, I felt insecure when my own views were challenged and quickly backed off if someone else was louder or more emphatic. At work, I could successfully argue cases before judges and juries because I wasn't representing my own causes or passions, but those of my clients. It was my professional duty to argue the facts of the case and the law that applied, but it wasn't personal.

Much to my surprise, that changed quickly after I became a mother. I finally found the motivation to meld my personal and political lives and speak up! If recent cocktail party conversations I've had with other mothers are any indication, I'm not alone. They have similar stories – it seems that there's something about motherhood that makes us feel a little more powerful when it comes to how we view the world we're going to leave to our children. For me, the combination of becoming a mom to a daughter and leaving the legal profession to return to my writing roots was empowering. I was able to focus on finding a more authentic path and a stronger activist voice.

You see, after our daughter arrived, I unexpectedly found myself out of work. The government agency position I held at the time was filled by a new Bush administration appointee when we returned home from our adoption trip to China. I was offered another slot, which would have required returning to the full-time practice of law – something I knew I didn't want. While I never intended to stop working or take an extended leave after I became a mother, I found I had an unexpected gift of time; I could step off my twenty-year professional track with my new baby and, between feedings and diaper changes, focus on what I really wanted to do with my life and what I could contribute.

Political thoughts percolated in my head! I realized I had enough experience under my belt to stick my toe in the waters of expressing my opinions without being afraid of how I might be challenged. I could be vocal about the changes for women that I had hoped would be a reality by the time I hit my forties but, sadly, were not. While my passion for politics started young, I didn't embrace the idea of a personal political life until I realized, looking at my daughter, that parenting would be one of the most political things I would ever do. Plus, I had the unexpected luxury of time to contemplate what life might look like for my daughter when she became an adult.

In my "spare" waking moments of new motherhood, I realized, in a way I hadn't when I was too busy with my sixty-hour-a-week work life, that things hadn't changed all that much for women. In those twenty-plus years between the time I started college and when I became a mother, I still made less money than many men in the same job, and less qualified men were still promoted ahead of me. (I can assure you I spent more time working on legal matters than my office mate did. He spent hours of phone time discussing the pizza business he ran on the side, yet my male supervisors saw fit to promote him first.) I got no paid maternity leave, and I was still expected to silently tolerate inappropriate jokes in the workplace, which drew no consequences for the joke tellers, while I was told to "have more of a sense of humor."

The thought of my daughter having to accept and tolerate a world that still looked like that made my blood boil.

Of course, the idea that motherhood is political is not new, even if it feels that way to us. Many of the suffragettes were mothers who fought not only for their own but also for their daughters' eventual right to vote. And as Cokie Roberts has written in her books about the early First Ladies, they were each political in their own way.

Even women who have spent years in the activist trenches have found motherhood to be politically re-energizing. Former NOW president Kim Gandy, a leading activist for two decades before she became a mother, told me that her commitment to the issues she was passionate about, including reproductive rights, exploded after she became a parent because she didn't want to see a world where the things she fought for weren't viewed as a birthright for her daughters.

U.S. Senator Amy Klobuchar from Minnesota often tells the story of how her political side came to the forefront after she was tossed out of the hospital 24 hours after delivering her daughter, who had a variety of medical issues at birth. As a result, Klobuchar, who was not then a public figure, mobilized her friends (many of them pregnant!) and made sure they were present at the hearings in her state about whether insurers should be required to allow new mothers to stay in the hospital for up to 48 hours. As she tells the story, the chances of that legislation getting passed in Minnesota didn't look good, but the pregnant women outnumbered the lobbyists present and they were able to convince the lawmakers otherwise. A wise lesson learned: you just don't get in the way of angry, activist pregnant women!

Reflecting on them, and on my own journey into motherhood, I got angry about the equal rights that were not yet a reality. I knew that if things were the same and women were still fighting against sexist treatment when my new daughter became a woman, I'd really feel that I had let the next generation down.

What if my ten-year-old is still fighting for equal pay when she's a woman? I wondered. When I was a teen, just clueing in to the realities of the world, I assumed we would be laughing today in disbelief that there once was a time when women earned less money than men for the same job. I believed that my NOW button that said "59¢" would be a quaint collector's item. Thirty years after wearing that button, I can't believe the current version says "77¢" and not "$1." I'd be willing to bet that pay-discrimination plaintiff Lilly Ledbetter probably felt the same way!

I had thought that by today, paid maternity leave and insurance-covered maternity care would be the rule not the exception, never envisioning anything like Republican Senator Jon Kyl's out-of-touch remarks during the 2009 health care debate, in which he said that insurance companies shouldn't be required to cover maternity care because he, as a man, had no need for such a thing in his policy. Thankfully, Democratic Senator Debbie Stabenow of Michigan was there to retort, "I think your mom probably did."

As I compared the world I predicted as a teen to the world I was actually raising my daughter in, I knew part of my job as a parent had to be trying to create the world I wished for her. But as only one person, who didn't hold political office or have connections to Capitol Hill power brokers, I wasn't sure what steps I could take. Other mothers I knew had similar questions about what to do next.

Blogging provides one answer. The opportunity to raise our voices online has created a powerful platform for thousands upon thousands of mothers: policymakers and legislators are starting to pay attention to those of us writing about politics and the issues we care about.

My blog, *PunditMom*, was born out of the need to share with others how my experiences as a mother shape my thoughts on public policy and political change, as well as the desire to bring other parents into the online conversations that I knew were going on privately. As a professional writer, I penned opinion pieces for over a year at a Washington, D.C. newspaper. It was an amazing opportunity to flex a little political muscle in a space that's dominated by testosterone! But when that freelance newspaper job ended, I knew that through blogging I had found a new way to discuss politics that resonated with me both as a woman and a parent. Back in the early days of blogging, I felt a bit alone as a political-mom commentator, but I hoped that if I kept at it and wrote about issues I cared about, others would join in. And they did. In the years since I started blogging, the number of parents writing about the change they want to see has grown significantly.

I still see so many smart, talented, savvy women who say they can't be political – that they don't know enough and worry that if they speak out they will get things wrong, others will attack them, or they will alienate friends who don't agree with their views. They lament that it takes too much time to read up on what's going on or that they don't have the time to pitch in for campaigns and rallies. But I would like to convince all mothers that despite the challenges of speaking up, we can't afford to sit on the sidelines any longer.

Women may find it more difficult to speak out than men because we're socialized from a very young age to be nice, polite girls, who don't interrupt, contradict others, or start fights. Consequently, our feelings get hurt when people disagree with us or challenge our opinions and actions. For example, both male and female attorneys often deal with nasty personal attacks from opposing counsel – that's one of the reasons I stopped practicing law. My mental and physical health suffered as a result of other attorneys using, for the benefit of their clients, whatever tactics they thought would wear me down, whether those means were approved by the rules of procedure or not. But for my attorney husband, enduring such behavior is just the price of doing business, and he ignores it. Other female former lawyers I've talked to say they've noticed this gender difference as well. And it's this same prospect of suffering personal attacks that keeps women afraid of expressing themselves online.

Given the current media environment, it's hard not to think of political writing or commentary as something that is potentially confrontational or meanspirited. After all, that has become the new wave in cable news. But with the communities parents have created online, there is an amazing opportunity to have our collective voices heard in new ways.

That's where our blogs come in. This still-new, grassroots platform has empowered us to put new ideas out there and, in some

cases, has turbocharged the process of finding our political voices
– it did for me, and it has for many others. Little by little, as
mothers publicly raise their concerns from their daily lives, they've
also found the power that their voices have in their burgeoning
political presence. Mothers are talking about food safety, toxic
plastics used in children's products, clean water, school systems,
problems navigating the health care system, "maternal profiling"
job discrimination, and so much more.

The collective power of mothers' voices online is huge and
being harnessed by grassroots organizations like MomsRising,
which co-founder Kristin Rowe-Finkbeiner discusses in detail
in the next chapter. In its work to create family-friendly public
policies, MomsRising gives parents opportunities to try on various political hats through letter-writing campaigns, petitions, and
group visits to lawmakers' offices.

In addition to *PunditMom*, more sites are coming online
that give mothers a forum to write about and discuss the policy
changes they believe are important, like *MOMocrats, Mother Talk-
ers, Help a Mother Out, Mothers Acting Up,* and others. Individual writers and mothers like Jill Miller Zimon of *Writes Like She
Talks,* Veronica Arreola of *Viva la Feminsta,* Morra Aarons-Mele
of *Women and Work,* and Tracee Sioux of *The Girl Revolution* are
writing political commentaries that rival anything you read in the
major newspapers.

But we need more women to add their voices to the mix. Political blog content is still predominantly written by men, leading a
November 2009 *Mother Jones* article to ask, somewhat dismissively,
"Where Are All the Lady Bloggers?" Although the gender repre-
sentation among blog writers is far from equal, there *are* women
writing. Perhaps the author missed the Summer 2009 *Ms. Magazine* article on the subject (advertised on the cover as "Mom 2.0:
She Blogs, She Tweets, She Rises Up!") or the coverage of women

bloggers meeting with White House senior advisor Valerie Jarrett at the 2009 BlogHer conference to discuss health care reform legislation that was being crafted and debated on Capitol Hill.

Concern for our children and the community binds us together. Whether we vote red, blue, or purple, many mothers discover their "political" voices through their children and parenting experiences. For many women, the political is uniquely personal and that personal connection drives their passion. For example, many mothers connect less through the abstract policy issues of the health care debate and more on the concrete impact policy has on the people they know and love. In the political world, our lawmakers are focused on the minutiae of crafting legislation and making deals; in the political worlds of mothers, we are motivated and inspired to write and become active when our loved ones are at risk.

I've been lucky enough to meet many mothers who write online about their lives, and many of them claim they are not political. I believed them at first, but after reading so much of their work, I don't buy it anymore. From the way they write about their lives, I recognize the same passion I feel about things that impact my life as a woman and a mother, whether they see themselves as political or not. They might be starting out slowly, but the political passion is there, even if they're still hesitant to use the "p" word!

Diana Prichard from *Of the Princess and the Pea* blog found her political voice to talk with her daughter about the reality of homelessness:

> During the close to six miles we walked [the day we went to Chicago], we passed quite a few homeless men and a couple of women with signs. I noticed The Princess' eyes lingering on them from the very first time we did. I could feel her hand, her steps slowing just slightly as we passed, everything I'd ever told her about some people not having homes or clothes or toys so

she must remain grateful coming to life. In her face, I could almost see the revelation. *Mom did not make this up. Those people don't have a home or clothes or toys. Oh. My. Gawd.*

Amie Adams of the *Mamma Loves . . .* blog got her political mojo on by writing about her outrage at Wall Street:

> Dear Failed Wall St. Financial Executives,
> We need to talk about your behavior . . .
>
> Millions of people have lost vast amounts of money . . . because of your actions. Bills will go unpaid causing other businesses to suffer. Those about to retire may now be looking at additional years of work when they should be enjoying the plans they had for their money that is now gone. Children will receive fewer presents this coming holiday season. Families will cancel vacations.
>
> Your bad behavior affects not only you but hundreds of millions of people too.
>
> When my kids misbehave they must face the consequences. How am I going to explain to them that when YOU misbehave the consequences aren't yours to face but theirs?

Sometimes the political is more about a state of mind – such as the rhetoric that Megan Jordan of the *Velveteen Mind* blog wrote about during the 2008 presidential campaign:

> The phrase "small town values" is being thrown around a lot lately. On one side of the aisle, you hear the declaration "We believe in small town values." On the other side, you hear the question, "But what *are* small town values" . . .

The question of small town values and whether or not they are relevant or important is intriguing, regardless of your political leanings. The majority of our country, if not our world, is small towns. Much of the populations of our cities migrated from small towns. Small-town America is the root of this country, so what does that mean to us?

There is no one definition of what "small town values" is, but to me it means a greater ability to see the people around you. Really *see* them.

One of my favorite commentators is Veronica Arreola, who blogs at *Viva La Feminista* and refers to herself as a "professional feminist" in her role directing a university program for women in science and engineering:

> I like to describe my job as being a grassroots organizer for women majoring in science and engineering. I have to herd them and sometimes bribe them with pizza. It's hard work.
>
> I also have to break their hearts and that's really the hardest part. When a student asks me why we don't have infant care. When a student asks me why a general science course is so "hard" and [why in some classes fifty percent will earn you a C unlike in high school]. The cold truths of academia break some of them and my job is to tell it like it is, but also instill some hope that if we all work together, maybe, just maybe things will change.
>
> And that's why I call myself a professional feminist. I'm not professional in that I'm churning out book after book. I'm not professional because I get paid thousands of dollars to speak (although if you want, just ask!). I'm

professional in that I get paid to work for educational and economic equity by supporting young women who want to be scientists and engineers.

While I was plenty political already in my thinking, I became even more so during the 2008 presidential campaign with the seemingly endless sexist media attacks on both Hillary Clinton and Sarah Palin. Reports about both women raised a myriad of issues that made me think, *Don't these people have daughters? And mothers and wives? Would they talk in front of their nieces or daughters about the cleavage of a national political figure or whether a mother of young children was an acceptable candidate for national office?* Online, I pondered aloud:

> Cleveland *Plain Dealer* columnist Connie Schultz wrote [during the campaign] "we bruise our daughters when we bash Hillary Clinton." She was generally talking about girls a bit older than the second-graders I sat with [at the school lunch table] . . . who were scarfing down chicken nuggets and jelly sandwiches, but the point is the same – our daughters are focused and invested in this presidential race because "a girl" – someone like them – wants to be in charge and make decisions.
>
> Girl power is a very big thing for our elementary school daughters.
>
> Since that's the case, we need to be careful how we describe Hillary because you can be sure that whatever we call Senator Clinton, our daughters are listening, and you know how girls find ways to internalize put-downs.

Some women whom I've tried to encourage to go out on a political limb – women who are amazingly confident and powerful writers – have gasped and physically withdrawn at the suggestion that they should put themselves out there in the realm of public opinion. The thought of such a thing is anathema to them, especially in our world of cable news "shouting heads." I don't blame them for thinking that cable news posturing does little to advance real debate, but I worry that we squelch our power when we are not willing to claim our right to be overtly political. It is one thing to not realize you are being political; another, to recoil from it.

So how do we convince more women, and mothers especially, that political expression doesn't have to be scary, and that it's important to voice our political feelings if we expect to create the world we wish for our children? And that, as American women, we have an obligation to speak out on issues from our place of relative political safety compared to other women around the world? We can't afford to remain silent and apolitical, because important decisions are being made, and politicians need to hear from us. Leaders like Amy Klobuchar and Debbie Stabenow need to know that we have their backs as they work to protect and advance our rights.

Overcoming our socialized aversion to being "political" doesn't have to be an all-or-nothing proposition. We can start one step at a time, supporting each other along the way, so that we do not let the fear of being criticized keep us from speaking up. And blogging offers a first step that just about anyone can try. Blogs are powerful because they offer a platform that is both widely accessible and influential. It's tough to break into the op-ed pages of *The New York Times* or *The Washington Post,* and in fact, women author only about one in six opinion pieces in national newspapers. But there is no barrier to entry in the blogosphere, which is giving women the outlet they have long needed to advocate for change. Increasing numbers of lawmakers are hiring social media directors to keep them tuned in to these online conversations, so online publishing is a growing opportunity to make our voices heard.

As we become more courageous in how we talk with others, including our children, about the "political" world and become more comfortable in our own political skins, we start to create a change in that world. Whether we're trying to raise the next generation of blue (borrowing a phrase from my fellow *MOMocrats*), or the next generation of red, or purple, we are raising the next generation of activists, policymakers, and voters. That requires us, as parents, to dig deep, be brave, and get in touch with our inner wonks.

We all have stories to share that bring out the "political" animals we have inside. Mothers are increasingly finding their political voices and taking action – whether it be writing online, signing a petition, getting a group of mothers together to meet with their local Congressional representative, or digging deep and deciding to run for office. The more our collective voices are heard, the more influence we can have as mothers.

Recently, I bought my fourth-grade daughter a T-shirt that says, "This is what a feminist looks like." My explanation of feminism to her was this – that girls could do or be anything that a boy could. As only a preteen girl can, she gave me her best eye roll and said, "Well, *DUH!*" A pretty simple political conversation, I confess. But if I have helped her in any way become at ease with her own views of the world by sharing mine and showing her that I'm not afraid to speak up about the things that are important to me, then I think I have done my job.

Building a Family-friendly America: Challenge and Progress Through the Eyes of MomsRising.org

Kristin Rowe-Finkbeiner

Kristin Rowe-Finkbeiner is Executive Director and co-founder of MomsRising.org, an online and on-the-ground grassroots organization of more than a million people who are working to achieve economic security for all families in the United States and to end discrimination against mothers. With MomsRising co-founder and President, Joan Blades, Kristin co-authored *The Motherhood Manifesto*. She also wrote the award-winning book *The F-Word: Feminism in Jeopardy*. In 2006, she was given an Excellence in Journalism award by the Society of Professional Journalists for magazine writing. Kristin has been deeply involved in cutting-edge politics, policy analysis, and grassroots organization for nearly two decades.

Despite all the rhetoric about being family-friendly, we have structured a society that is profoundly family-unfriendly . . . What's missing right now is a movement. What's missing is mobilization, and that's why MomsRising is so important.

⁓ Senator Barack Obama, September 2006

A LEGACY OF ACTIVISM FOR CHANGE

I wear a ring on my left hand, just above my wedding band and engagement ring. This ring was given to my mother by my grandmother, and to my grandmother by my great-grandmother. A simple gold band with engraved initials and etched circular swooping lines, this ring is one part of the trifecta of past, present, and future that I carry with me as I type, work, raise children, and go through my days.

Through MomsRising.org, a nonprofit organization I co-founded with Joan Blades in 2006 to empower moms and people who love them to fight for family economic security and to end discrimination against mothers, we're building upon the legacy of the women's rights activists who came before us. That's right. Standing on the shoulders of giants, we've grown to over a million members working together in a grassroots movement. Whether we are collaborating online or on the ground, MomsRising's work is centered in a continuum of activism done by both the heroines in our past and by our allies who are now fighting alongside us for women's rights.

My ring reminds me, each and every day, of the women who came before us. This ring was given to my grandmother by my great-grandmother – a great-grandmother who was the first president of the Rochester, New York Planned Parenthood chapter, in the time of Susan B. Anthony.

My grandmother remembers her mother teaching women about birth control – in a time when only "people of ill repute" did such a thing – and standing tall in the face of priests banging loudly at the door in protest.

The ring was then passed down from my grandmother (who later took over that Rochester Planned Parenthood presidency) to my mother, a strong feminist in her own right who worked for many years as a social worker for Prince Georges County Family Services, and then finally to me when I turned 16.

The ring is an ever-present historical anchoring for me, reminding me that women in our nation only got the right to vote in 1920. That's just ninety years ago – less than one lifetime.

My great-grandmother's heirloom reminds me that due to the hard work of the women before us, incredible battles have been won, and barriers to equality have been broken down. Successes such as the landmark Civil Rights Act of 1964 (Title VII), which banned employment discrimination based on race, sex, religion, or national origin, created turning points for women in the workplace.

These wins place us where we are today.

The ring I wear reminds me that all of us in our nation come from a long line of women for whom the responsibility of civic engagement to better our nation was a given, and for whom the inequalities faced by women were walls to be broken down. And while some walls have been demolished, many are still standing tall.

Right now, in our modern times, one of the biggest barriers to equality – impacting all 83 million mothers in our nation and the families they are raising – is smack dab in the center of motherhood. We at MomsRising call this the "Maternal Wall."

THE MATERNAL WALL

The "glass ceiling" is often the first thing that comes to mind when people talk about modern women's inequality in the workplace. (To be sure, the glass ceiling is still quite solid. Right now there are only 15 women CEOs at Fortune 500 companies.) Yet there is another barrier to career advancement that often keeps mothers from even getting near the glass ceiling in the first place: the Maternal Wall.

Since over eighty percent of women in the United States have children by the time they are 44 years old, the majority of American women will be affected by this invisible Wall that inhibits hiring, promotion, and equal pay. Due to the advancements made by our mothers, grandmothers, and great-grandmothers, many young women today may not be aware of gender discrimination until they become mothers. The Maternal Wall is a pivotal challenge of modern feminism.

Here's what that Maternal Wall looks like: women without children make about 90 cents to a man's dollar, women with children make about 73 cents, and single moms make only about 60 cents to each dollar earned by a man. Sociologist Shelley Correll's 2005 experimental research found that given otherwise equal resumes, mothers were 79 percent less likely to be hired than women without children. When moms were recommended for hire, they were offered an average of $11,000 lower starting salaries. (Dads, on the other hand, were offered $6,000 higher starting salaries than non-dads.) In addition, Correll found that moms were judged by harsher standards in the workplace; for instance, moms were taken off the management track for fewer late days than non-moms.

What's going on here? Why is the Maternal Wall so tall right now? Times have changed, but our family economic security policies are stuck in the 1950s, when many families had a parent at home. That's just not the case today.

Women are now half of the entire paid labor force in the United States, and while three-quarters of mothers are in the labor force, mothers still get paid less for the same job as an equally qualified man (or woman without children).

The Maternal Wall begins to explain why so many women and children are living in poverty, why still so few women are in national leadership, and why not enough children are getting the healthy starts they need.

There are solutions. There are critically important policies for family economic security which must be passed to catch our nation up with modern times – policies like paid family leave, sick days and health care, access to early-learning and after-school opportunities, and fair pay. It should be noted that the majority of other industrialized nations have such policies. For example, a Harvard study found that paid family leave is available for new moms in all but four of the over 170 countries evaluated. The four countries without this policy are Papua New Guinea, Liberia, Swaziland, and, yes, the United States of America.

Such family-friendly policies are long overdue here in the United States, and will – when passed – put a big dent in the Maternal Wall. You see, studies of other countries show that passing family economic security policies can actually narrow the wage gap between mothers and non-mothers.

Solutions are indeed possible. We can break down the Maternal Wall.

THE MOMSRISING.ORG STORY

My journey toward the movement that would become MomsRising started over ten years ago when I had my first child, who was beautiful, glorious, and very, very sick with a primary immuno-deficiency syndrome.

I was married, 26 years old, and the Political and Field Director of a state environmental PAC; I was expecting to go right back to work – like most mothers do these days.

I hadn't planned for this particular twist in my life path.

When I say my son was sick, I mean sick: he had an immune deficiency that left him extremely vulnerable to infections. A minor cold meant hospital trips, weeks- or even months-long antibiotic treatments, steroids, sometimes more than seven drugs at a time, and too often a child fighting pneumonia and struggling to breathe.

My son couldn't be in child care because the other kids would get him sick. There was no choice but for me to leave full-time work.

Since I myself wasn't raised in a two-parent household, I couldn't help but think of the "what ifs" that went with my particular situation: *What if I didn't have a husband whose job provided health care coverage for our family? What if we couldn't rely on his pay to put food on our table and a roof over our heads?*

There simply isn't a safety net.

My son is now a healthy, strong young man whose immune system more fully developed as he grew older, but this experience opened my eyes to just how close to the economic edge so many mothers, children, and families are in our nation.

When I finally raised my head up from taking care of a child who was struggling to breathe, I couldn't help but think of all the other families who found themselves in similar situations, but who, *through no fault of their own*, weren't set up to weather an unexpected crisis.

And I did what any normal political numbers geek would do: I called the U.S. Census Bureau. I had to know just how many people like me there were out there. But when I asked a staffer at the Bureau's public information office how many stay-at-home moms there were in America, he said they didn't know. They didn't track unpaid labor, so they weren't tracking full-time moms – and still don't.

This was huge. The U.S. Census is used for government and business planning – and full-time moms were invisible!

Invisible.

I kept looking for answers and next called the Bureau of Labor Statistics (as directed by the good folks at the Census Bureau). Let me just say that it's a telling sign that a public information economist from the

Bureau of Labor Statistics told me, "We don't specifically track stay-at-home moms because they aren't relevant to the labor force."

Not relevant? Imagine the uproar if the government decided to call any other segment of the population irrelevant. The absence of full-time parents in U.S. Census data is especially disconcerting because the census is supposed to provide a snapshot of American life that drives public funding, political policy, consumer marketing, and much more. The federal government uses census data to allocate funds for economically disadvantaged persons, job training, public assistance programs, and other services. The private sector uses the same data to help in formulating marketing plans, developing products, and selecting office and plant sites. Legislative bodies use census data to develop laws to assist underrepresented groups and for community planning. Invisibility in the census thus has rippling repercussions and long-term financial consequences.

As of 2010, there still aren't any plans to ask a question about full-time parenthood on the U.S. Census.

I continued researching. I kept pulling on the string of startling facts, and, like a magician's scarf, it seemed to never end. My worldview was changing as the research piled up in folders on my desk. Until I had children, I mistakenly thought that the women who came before me – women like my great-grandmother, grandmother, and mother – had mostly accomplished the fight for women's rights issues in our nation. But as more and more data emerged, I realized that the fight for equality was far from over.

I picked up the baton.

Incensed by the invisibility and economic vulnerability of moms, I started writing magazine articles about these issues, eventually writing a book about the current state of women's equality in our nation, *The F-word: Feminism in Jeopardy – Women, Politics, and the Future*. In my articles and book, I shine a spotlight on a mountain of facts showing that motherhood was (and still is today) the key modern barrier to women's equality and economic security in our nation. (And remember, over eighty percent of women in America become mothers by the time they are 44 years old, so the vast majority of women are impacted.)

Motherhood is too often a fast track to economic insecurity for both mothers and their children. Women who become mothers suffer compounding economic consequences: lower pay, hiring discrimination, and a significantly greater likelihood of living in poverty at some point in their lives. After all, it's no coincidence that a quarter of families with young children are living in poverty or that the USDA's November 2009 report shows that nearly one in four American children experience hunger multiple times a year. This is a direct outcome of the economic effects women experience when they become mothers.

So when Joan Blades, co-founder of the civic engagement organization MoveOn.org, asked me to join her in writing a book about the need for family-friendly public policies and a change of work culture, I enthusiastically agreed.

The resulting book, *The Motherhood Manifesto: What America's Moms Want – and What to Do About It,* describes the inequities of motherhood and the government and workplace policies that need to change so that women, mothers, and families have increased family economic security. But after uncovering so many unsettling facts and interviewing so many struggling families, Joan and I knew that our involvement with these issues couldn't end when the book was published. *The Motherhood Manifesto* was a call to action, and MomsRising was our answer.

SOCIETY NEEDS M.O.T.H.E.R.S.

At MomsRising, each day we hear new stories of mothers all over the country who are struggling to raise kids despite backwards policies, reminding us all that we don't have an epidemic of personal failings, but instead a national, structural problem which we must address together. Stories like those of Kiki Peppard, who moved from New York to Pennsylvania in 1994 and lined up more than a dozen job interviews before she was offered a position. Interview after interview ended abruptly when the employer asked if she was married or had children, and Kiki answered truthfully that she was a single mother. Some employers blatantly told her that the company "didn't hire mothers because they took too much time off of work." The stories of women like Kiki remind us all that there is still work to be done. (Indeed, over a decade and a half later, Kiki is *still* working to change Pennsylvania law to protect mothers from employment discrimination.)

Likewise, the hopeful stories of other mothers lucky enough to be in workplaces that "get it" remind us that the policy changes we seek are not only possible, they are beneficial to corporate bottom lines. In fact, recent studies show that companies with women in leadership are actually doing better fiscally in this tough economic environment. For example, a Pepperdine University study found that in 2008, Fortune 500 companies that are most attractive to businesswomen fiscally outperformed industry medians on every measure; profits as a percent of revenue were 15% higher, profits as a percent of assets were 32% higher, and profits as a percent of equity was 31% higher.

If we're going to break down the Maternal Wall, we as a movement have our work cut out for us. MomsRising uses the acronym M.O.T.H.E.R.S. as shorthand to communicate the focus of our advocacy toward breaking down that wall – all the while never forgetting the real women and families that are behind each letter:

M = Maternity/Paternity Leave, Paid

Making families choose between spending adequate time with a new baby and facing financial ruin is not a real choice, and it's bad social policy. Mothers like Selena Allen, who had her baby on a Thursday and was back at work on Monday while her newborn was in the neonatal ICU, shouldn't have to decide between taking unpaid time off to recover from birth and be with her preemie son, or putting food on the table. Paid family leave is associated with lower infant mortality rates and savings for employers due to lower employee turnover.

O = Open, Flexible Workplaces

Mothers need the flexibility to structure their jobs in a way that complements their family life. Allowing flexible work options is a win-win. Both small and large businesses, from moving companies to software corporations, find that flexible scheduling attracts and retains highly qualified workers, increases employee productivity and performance, and lowers turnover-related costs.

T = TV We Choose and After-School Programs

Families need the support of free or low-cost after-school programs that provide enrichment, safety, and supervision, as well as more quality television programming choices that offer viewers an alternative to the hyper-violent, ad-messaging-laden norm. The city of Seattle has found that for every $1 spent on quality after-school programming, the community sees a return of nearly $13 in student improvement and reduced juvenile delinquency.

H = Health Care for All Kids

Many families are uninsured or underinsured. Even families lucky enough to have insurance, like Arnold and Sharon Dorsett, can find themselves unable to keep up with the high cost of health care. The Dorsetts had to declare bankruptcy when they were unable to pay their son Zachary's $10,000–$20,000 per year medical bills – their ten percent portion of his total treatment costs. Medical debt is a factor in half of all bankruptcies, and parents should not have to face financial insolvency to care for an ill child.

E = Early Care and Education

All families need access to excellent child care, yet too often the care kids need isn't affordable, accessible, or up to the quality standards that would prepare children for kindergarten. In our contemporary culture, most mothers need to return to the workplace before their children are in elementary school, and many do not have child care support from relatives. With child care costing between $4,000 and $10,000 per child per year, many families are struggling to make ends meet. Investments in quality early care and education result in societal savings by producing children who are, as adults, more likely to be employed or enrolled in school and less likely to be receiving welfare benefits or have a criminal record.

R = Realistic, Fair Wages

Mothers need to be able to financially support their families. Women make up the majority of minimum wage workers, who, despite working full-time, often need to utilize government benefit programs to meet their basic needs. Not only do mothers need livable wages, they need fair wages: as I mentioned earlier, Shelley Correll's research shows that mothers are offered an average of $11,000 less in annual starting salary than equally qualified women without children.

S = Sick Days for All, Paid

The United States is the only industrialized country that doesn't guarantee all workers a minimum number of paid sick days. Without the protection of paid sick days, many moms have lost needed income, or even their jobs, because they got sick or because they took time off to be with their ill children.

MOMSRISING.ORG MAKES IT EASY TO TAKE ACTION

There's one thing we all know: the voices of mothers are powerful. Working together, we can indeed move mountains, much less policy. After toilet training a two-year-old, taking on corporate lobbyists is not very difficult.

MomsRising.org is using the power of moms, reaching out to busy people online and in person, to work toward breaking down the Maternal Wall. We engage mothers with an agenda that crosses social, cultural, and economic divides and welcome those who have never before participated in political change. One of our members named Kymberlee told us how she felt about getting involved: "Thank you, MomsRising, for giving me the courage to call our state legislators for the first time, during my lunch hour. I never dreamed I could fit lobbying into my busy schedule! I cannot wait to start seeing the amazing impact this bill will have."

MomsRising's successes thus far are due to our commitment to connect with members in the ways that work best for them. In addition to using tried and true on-the-ground organizing tactics, we engage members through phone, email, text messages, blogs, Twitter, Facebook, and other social media. We constantly listen to the top issues of our members and pick those issues up when there is enough momentum to "ride the waves of change."

Why is this type of multiple-approach citizen engagement so important right now? A key reason is that we live in a dynamic, hectic environment where ever-busier Americans work more hours per week than workers in most any other nation, and each person receives a total of over three thousand direct and indirect media marketing messages per day. It's becoming harder and harder to break through this static to have our voices heard.

On the positive side, new doors are opening. Emerging technology platforms offer new political tactics and an increasing number of ways for citizens to become politically engaged.

We see it as our job at MomsRising to bring our members as many tools as possible to break through the communications static we each are bathed in every day to have their voices heard by key decision makers. Fortunately, today's new version of political engagement includes a continuum of opportunities, from joining an online community that matches one's values and beliefs, to sharing personal stories and support, to attending an in-person meeting at a U.S. Senator's office. Today, electoral engagement, legislative advocacy, and actions toward cultural change can easily be broken down into small pieces; anyone can have an impact from a living room chair in the time between getting home from work and eating dinner. The choice for where to spend precious citizen engagement time is in the hands of each of our members. Our job at MomsRising is to open as many avenues as possible for people to have their voices heard, so people can choose from a menu of engagement options to find those that fit in their busy lives.

MomsRising believes that in our harried modern world, it can be very powerful – and is often necessary – to use as many advocacy strategies as possible at the same time in order to most effectively have our voices heard. These include face-to-face tools such as direct lobbying for legislation, constituent contacts with policy-makers, fundraising parties, protests, and voting; education tools such as citizen leadership development, research, and best practices outreach to business owners; Internet and technology tools such as cell phone and email campaigns, blogs, social networks, and online dialogues; and artistic tools such as music, humor, and video. MomsRising leverages the combined use of these tools to end discrimination against mothers and build a nation where children, parents, and businesses can thrive.

MOMS ARE POWERFUL AND MAKING CHANGES

Working strategically with MomsRising's over one million members and key policy partners from over one hundred aligned organizations has proven to be remarkably effective. MomsRising is advancing important family issues to the forefront of the country's awareness and breaking the logjam that has been holding back family-friendly policies for decades. Working in coalition with other organizations, MomsRising has already helped achieve many recent successes.

Fair pay. MomsRising provided the grassroots support, in collaboration with aligned organizations, to make the Lilly Ledbetter Fair Pay Act the first piece of legislation signed into law by President Obama. Our members used creative tactics to raise awareness of the need for fair pay, including sending over ten thousand resumes to Senator John McCain to counter his statement that what women really need is not protection from discrimination but more education and training. These resumes were then printed and delivered to the Senator's office by local MomsRising members wearing sashes that read "Magnificently Overqualified Mothers" to demonstrate the level of education and training that American moms already have. The press had a field day. In recognition of the work MomsRising members did educating the nation about the need for such a law, MomsRising was invited to the Fair Pay Act bill signing at the White House.

Paid family leave. We are moving forward on the issue of paid family leave at the state and national level. In the states of Washington and New Jersey, members sent tens of thousands of emails, submitted letters to the editors of local papers, staged press events, delivered fortune cookies with key messages, sent in pictures of their children, held educational house parties, and made "mom visits" to each and every legislator to talk about their own family's need for this policy. This work has been widely recognized for its key role in helping these states become the second and third states in the nation (after California) to pass paid family leave policies.

Children's health care. We worked with First Focus, the National Council of La Raza, Families USA, and others to expand health care coverage to four million additional children and end the five-year waiting period for immigrant children under the Children's Health Insurance Program (CHIPRA). Our members shared their personal health care stories, educated their mom communities by blogging about the need for kids' coverage, sent letters to the newspaper editors in their communities, handed out stickers at presidential debates, and sent tens of thousands of letters to their representatives.

Unemployment insurance. We joined the National Employment Law Center and other policy partners to educate mothers and leaders about the lack of unemployment insurance for part-time and low-wage workers. Our support and education helped to win passage of the Unemployment Insurance Modernization Act. Already, 25 states have taken advantage of this legislation to expand unemployment insurance to these workers.

Child care and early learning. Along with the National Women's Law Center, First Focus, and other allies, we worked to ensure that

increases in funding for child care and Head Start and improve-
ments to the child tax credit to benefit low-income families were
included in the American Recovery and Reinvestment Act.

Product safety and environmental health. We continue to educate
the public about the need to ban the toxic plastics additive bisphe-
nol-A (BPA) in baby bottles and stop the use of other toxins in baby
products and toys that affect the health of our families. MomsRising was recognized in *The Washington Post* as being a major force
behind the successful pressuring of major retailers to stop selling
baby bottles that contained BPA. Additionally, we worked successfully with the Breast Cancer Fund and other environmental
groups to create the public pressure needed for both houses of
Congress to pass the Consumer Products Safety Improvement Act
in 2008 – enacting the toughest lead standards in the world and
banning six phthalates from children's products. President Bush
signed this legislation into law on August 14, 2008.

SPEAKING UP IS ESSENTIAL

My great-grandmother knew that if she stayed silent, many
women in her community might not have found the help they
needed to take control over their reproductive lives. My great-
grandmother knew that she couldn't wait for someone else to act
on her convictions. And it is the same with the family-friendly
M.O.T.H.E.R.S. policies – moms need help *now*.

As half of the labor force and slightly over half of the elector-
ate, women have come a long way and pack an increasingly powerful political punch. But we haven't arrived yet. We still must use
our collective political power to fight for family-friendly policies
like paid family leave, affordable child care, fair pay laws, health
care for all, flexible work options, and paid sick days – policies
which are the norm in most other industrialized nations. Passing

these policies is particularly important because studies show that they will ease the wage gaps and help everyone with both the fiscal and family bottom lines – businesses, parents, and non-parents alike. These are the very policies we need to break down the Maternal Wall.

We must act quickly. Times are tough, and getting tougher for mothers and families. With the November 2009 USDA announcement that one in four children in our nation are on the brink of hunger, we have little time to waste. Particularly since on the equality front we're not moving forward, we're falling behind. According to the World Economic Forum's 2009 international gender equality rankings, the United States fell four spots from last year. We now stand at 31st place, just behind Lithuania.

The time to act is now.

Whether you join us at MomsRising.org or act in another way, you cannot wait for someone else to act on your behalf, because this movement needs everyone's voice. If you are a mother, or if you *have* a mother, you can help America enact public policies that bring economic security for those of us on Main Street, not just Wall Street.

Together we can knock down the Maternal Wall and level the playing field for our daughters and sons. All it takes is each of us giving a little extra time for civic engagement wedged into the juggling act that is modern parenthood. Working with MomsRising has shown me more than anything that mothers have a powerful voice.

Because of this power, we together hold the future in our hands. It's a future we build every day, intentionally or not, as we raise our children and make choices about what to do with our own time and energy. Making the choice to spend some time each week deliberately shaping the direction of our state and nation toward better family economic security can take very little time for each of us on a day-to-day basis. But by each of us taking a bit of time each week, along with the rest of our members – and moms across the nation – taking a bit of time each week, together we'll have a lasting impact on future generations.

Yes, together, all of our efforts, small and large, will go a long way toward toppling the Maternal Wall so that our children have better economic security when they raise their children.

I can't wait to see the world in which my son raises his children, and to see my ring on my daughter's finger one day as she raises her own children in a nation that does better by women and families than we do today.

It Takes a Motherhood

Cooper Munroe and Emily McKhann

Emily McKhann and Cooper Munroe are the founders of the award-winning community for moms, www.TheMotherhood.com.

Here's a fun fact – the word *courage* comes from the French word for heart, *coeur,* so it actually means "the ability to stand by one's heart or one's core."

The way we see it, to tap our own courageousness, we must get to the heart of what matters to us and find our voice from there.

We are the founders of a Web community for mothers called TheMotherhood.com, where finding one's center – and the courage that goes with it – comes through receiving the input, help, and support of other moms.

Every day in TheMotherhood.com, women turn to each other for support, to say, "Oh hon, I've so been there," or "I've got an idea for you to think about," or "You go, girl!" or even just, "I hear you."

That's how it's been for us. Moms on the Web have been the wind at our backs and have given us the courage to build the online neighborhood of our maternal dreams.

We never in a million years would have predicted this path for ourselves, but glancing in the rear-view mirror now, we can see that our entire journey has led us here, exactly where we are meant to be.

Back in 2004 (we've worked together on and off for twenty years now), we set out to write a book about "parenting in the big picture," and early on decided to try out blogging to brainstorm content and gather feedback for the book. We called our blog *Been There.*

We had no idea what would unfold: how we would get to know amazing mothers who were also blogging, and how often they would write just what we each needed to hear at any given moment. Over and over, as we read blogs by moms and dads who had "been there" too, we found support, understanding, laughs, and insight, and were completely blown away by the power of it all.

Our lives took a decided turn when the levees broke in New Orleans after Hurricane Katrina and we converted our blog into a grassroots donation bulletin board, the *Been There Clearinghouse.* Thanks to our readers (mostly moms) getting the word out, thousands upon thousands of people started coming to the site. The donors and recipients (again mostly moms) came from all walks of life.

Our Clearinghouse went on to win the Best of Blogs Award for Most Inspirational Blog of 2005. We made deep and lasting connections with the many mothers and others who told their stories, gave of themselves, and found inspiration through the Clearinghouse.

The Clearinghouse opened our eyes to the fact that mothers

are phenomenal at supporting each other through whatever challenges they face. We saw the strength and courage that mothers took from their shared stories and interactions. During those long days, seeing how the give and take of online conversations changed peoples' lives often brought us to tears.

From there, it was the most natural thing in the world to create an online community – TheMotherhood.com – and with the encouragement of the many moms we met online, it actually felt doable to create a new Web neighborhood while raising young kids.

Our goal was to create a community where mothers could talk, listen, be there for each other, and get awesome ideas and help, whenever they had the time and wherever they were. We didn't realize that along the way, all that goodness from the community would be just what we needed to have the courage and faith to keep going. It was a classic example of wanting to do something for others, only to realize that we were the lucky ones to get to be with – and be inspired and encouraged by – these great women.

When we say *coeur* is at the center of everything that happens in TheMotherhood, we're speaking of our own journeys and what we see the community members offering up for one another every day. Which is why we knew, when Amy asked us to contribute a chapter to this book, that the moms in TheMotherhood.com had to be a part of it, too.

To gather the wisdom of TheMotherhood, we scheduled a time and invited the community and this anthology's contributors to join us for a live text chat on the topic of what it means to be a courageous parent. (You can read the archived chat at www.themotherhood.com/circlechat.php?l=58551.)

As you might imagine, a dynamic, rich, eye-opening conversation developed as we explored what being a "courageous parent" meant to each of us.

WHAT WE LEARNED

Everyone, even the most seasoned expert, needs a bit of courage, especially when it comes to parenting. It can take a huge amount of courage to confront some of the most basic challenges we regularly face:

> To stop thinking it all has to get done at once – perfectly
>
> To feel confident in our parenting decisions and beliefs
>
> To be fully in the moment
>
> To stand up for ourselves and our kids
>
> To ask for help
>
> To stop feeling guilty
>
> To not feel overwhelmed
>
> To not be weighed down by judgmental people
>
> To get out of our own way
>
> To not become isolated
>
> To learn more about ourselves
>
> To see the forest through the trees
>
> To follow our *hearts*

Why is it so hard to find the courage to overcome these ubiquitous parenting roadblocks?

Media Influences

Mainstream media isn't helping us. Family life is portrayed in such a negative light in articles, television programs, and studies that one might think the American family is distinguished only by its dysfunction.

> The media is invested in making us feel anxious, creating problems, and then selling the solutions back to us.
>
> ~ Amy Tiemann, *Courageous Parents, Confident Kids* editor

We all know this. Study after study tells us: babies aren't stim-ulated enough; math scores are down; colleges won't accept our kids unless they're in a gazillion extracurricular activities starting at age five; and we shouldn't tell our children they did a "good job" on anything because we will damage their self-esteem *for-ever*. But wait. We are also told our kids are also over-scheduled, overstimulated, need to be bored, and should convene with nature daily.

> Sometimes all it takes for me is a reminder of what I've managed to do RIGHT. My kids may not be Rhodes scholars, but they try hard in school; they may not be star soccer players, but they're kind and polite. Some-times all I see are the areas where I think I'm falling short as a parent. Being reminded of the ways I've done right by my kids encourages me to keep trying.
>
> ⁓ Becki, TheMotherhood.com member

Even when we rationally know that some alarmist advice has dubious value, it can sneak past our analytic minds and hit our emotions, making us feel inadequate or guilty.

> The bad things that happen to kids are publicized to the point that we consider ourselves responsible parents if we're keeping all those things in mind. There's this feel-ing that kids have to be supervised walking to the bus stop and then waiting for the bus because of potential kid swiping – even though the reality of this is so small. I was given an enormous amount of freedom as a child and try to give that to my kids as well, but it's hard to trust that they're going to make good choices and the world isn't a terrible place.
>
> ⁓ Maggie Chotas, TheMotherhood.com member

Keeping the Big Picture in View

What also came through loud and clear in our talk in TheMother-hood.com was this: there are so many reasons we aren't getting to the heart of the matter and finding the courage we need as parents.

We live in a climate where it is easy to get caught up in the minutiae of daily life and let outside pressures, expectations, and bumps in the road prevent us from living out what we want – what we really, truly, honestly want – for ourselves and our families.

Where is the big-picture perspective? Where is that forest through the trees?

> I used to be two different moms – a public mom and a private mom. The public mom was always smiling, always laughing, never yelled, always had her stuff to-gether, always – well – perfect (but you know, not real-ly). Then we'd get home and I would become this yelly, overwhelmed, crazy mom. Why? Because I couldn't keep the act up. I pulled it off for a bit before it all started to crumble.
>
> Because there is only so long you can keep up those sorts of acts before you start to crack. It was hard to work through. Not being perfect filled me with a lot of anxi-ety – that I would screw up my kids, that they would grow up not liking me, that other people wouldn't like me, that something bad would happen to the kids or to me, and somehow pretending to be perfect and put together would prevent all of that.
>
> And yet, all it really did was make me crazy and probably my daughter wished we lived in public all the time because at home, I was a mess!

For me, being courageous is all about being authentic and true to myself, even if it's not being perfect or doing what everyone else is doing. And a huge part of it is trusting MY instincts. Because with my first [child] I did a lot of what I thought I was supposed to do, even when it went against what I felt I should be doing.

I've truly come to learn, there is no right way to be a perfect parent, but a million ways to be a good parent. And I've also learned that I don't want to be perfect. It's too hard. It's too much stress, it's too much anxiety. I'm *110%* happy with being a good parent.

⁓ Brandie, TheMotherhood.com member

We've got our never-ending to-do lists, and we're there for everyone around us – our kids, partners, aging parents, bosses, co-workers, friends, neighbors, community groups – handling problems as they arise, finding solutions, doing our jobs, juggling it all, holding everything together.

We plan out our lives – plot careers, organize events, schedule vacations, plan for retirement – but we struggle to find balance for ourselves and our families in the day-to-day.

We're overwhelmed most days with all there is to do. And catching our breath? Forget it.

No one in the paid workforce is expected to *24/7*, live where they work, be constantly surrounded by the people they work with . . . Many people, including [stay-at-home moms] themselves, think [they] don't work, hence they don't deserve a vacation, can't expect their husbands to put the kids to bed, etc.

⁓ Melissa Stanton, *Courageous Parents, Confident Kids*
contributor

Even with all this noise swirling around us about what's right and wrong for kids and families, in our hearts, each of knows what holds true for our own families. Sometimes we feel we have easy access to that knowledge, and other times – most of the time – we feel cut off from any sense of what's going to work for us because we can't find the "quiet" to think it through or even identify it.

One of the biggest obstacles we heard to finding courage is, of course, finding time.

The sign of the times is . . . we don't have time.

> Sometimes it seems that life does not allow us (or we don't allow ourselves) the time and quiet to just stop and really consider. Laundry must get done, dinner cooked, that sales report written, that permission slip signed. It feels like an unaffordable luxury to just slip away and think – but it's really a critical necessity.
>
> ∼ Becki, TheMotherhood.com member

Add to that not having enough support, feeling external and internal pressure to do it all, feeling guilt about just about every-thing, having unreachable expectations, and seeing media and judgment all around us. All this together makes it hard, really hard, to put ourselves first, connect the dots, and get to the heart of things.

> Life isn't about one-size-fits-all solutions and these stud-ies often frame things as black and white instead of the infinite shades of gray. I find that I'm empowered when I seek discussions about alternatives that have worked for different people, instead of discussions that focus on the problems.
>
> ∼ Maryanne Perrin, *Courageous Parents, Confident Kids*
> contributor

Finding Community in Motherhood

It takes a lot of courage, but one of the most important things we need to do for ourselves and each other is *figure out a way to give ourselves a break.*

We have the toughest job under the sun. And, yet, we beat ourselves up, we beat each other up, and we can't open a newspaper without being reminded what slackers we are.

Here's an idea – it came up several times in the chat in TheMotherhood.com (and science is on our side on this too):

What about actively and intentionally taking care of each other, being a community, and sharing our stories, ups and downs, and progress along the way? It turns out this is one of the most effective strategies – and it's also very, very good for us.

Dr. Allie Domar, who runs the Domar Center for Mind/Body Health, made waves when she proved that mind/body techniques and support groups can help women get pregnant. Other scientific studies have shown that women supporting each other improves the life expectancy for breast cancer patients and reduces the impact of conditions like migraines and heart disease.

Translation: taking care of ourselves by talking with other women – expressing our feelings and connecting on an emotional level – contributes to our health and well-being in a scientifically proven way.

> Our moms were so strongly bound to an Asian cultural notion of mother-martyr, and . . . that didn't help us as little girls (I felt guilty about all she gave up to raise me.) My goal . . . is to show my girls that I take care of them by taking care of myself – giving myself time to exercise, to follow my interests, to keep learning without shame from both failure and success, every single day of my life.
>
> ～ Zephyr, TheMotherhood.com member

My husband lived out of state during the week when I was on bed rest with my twins, and for seven months after they arrived. I was also caring for our first-born, then a preschooler. My girlfriends and neighbors literally took care of me. At that time in my life I was able to depend on them more than I could my spouse, my parents, or in-laws. The experience also showed which of my friends and family I could rely on, and which ones I couldn't. Some women I knew only in passing offered their help, which I accepted. I made many new, and lasting, friends.

> ∽ Melissa Stanton, *Courageous Parents, Confident Kids* contributor

Tips for Bringing Out Your Courageous Parent

We discussed community support and several additional solutions throughout the course of our chat, and we'll let some of the participants tell you in their own words how they find courage as parents:

Work together

> In the United States, we have such a do-it-yourself culture that we resist the notion that joining forces is actually beneficial for everyone – moms and kids and everyone involved.
>
> ∽ Maya Frost, *Courageous Parents, Confident Kids* contributor

Ask for help

> Learning to ask for and receive help changed my life so radically after having my son Jonah. But yes, it's hard when it goes against our very independent-focused culture and when we're so busy. But the research on

women/friendship is so compelling – we are literally changed physiologically when we gather to support and empower one another (we release serotonin among other things!).

~ Renee Trudeau, *Courageous Parents, Confident Kids* contributor

Train yourself to find the time – yes, like a marathon: start with short periods and work your way up

. . . I think [self-nurturing] needs to be LEARNED and PRACTICED, at first. There are so many societal pressures for mothers to be selfless givers all the time that I think we have to consciously, purposely decide and learn HOW to take care of ourselves. But I found that once I got the hang of it, I REALLY liked it. I definitely don't have to struggle to do nice things for myself anymore! :-)

~ Patty Ayers, *Courageous Parents, Confident Kids* project manager

Challenge yourself to go outside your comfort zone

I co-facilitate a support group for parents who have adopted their children through the foster care system. Many are still giddy with fresh newborns, others are working through big issues, behaviorally, emotionally, etc. I think I would not get much from a group where all the parents seemed perfect.

We struggle – many of us daily – and yet we look to each other for solutions and for advocacy ideas. Many of our children have special needs and we problem solve together . . . which for me sums up courageous parenting. Working together to raise a child as a village.

Because as old as that saying may be and as often as you hear it takes a village to raise a child, some children, let me tell you . . . require an awful lot of the villagers. But it's worth it.

~ Thriftymommastips, TheMotherhood.com member

Be truthful with yourself and others

The problem is also that we're afraid of admitting – to ourselves and others – truths that make us seem like rotten moms, e.g., some stay-at-home moms don't like being 24/7 caregivers. Some employed moms work because they don't want to be home with kids all day, and they want to earn money and have a big career and family, just like men do. Many [moms are] so thankful to learn that they [aren't] alone in their "less-than-perfect" feelings about motherhood.

~ Melissa Stanton, *Courageous Parents, Confident Kids* contributor

Keep at it

Don't you think this is one area that busy moms let fall to the side? "I'm too busy to join a support group, have lunch with my friends, etc." One more example of not placing your mojo high enough on the priority list.

~ Amy McCready, *Courageous Parents, Confident Kids* contributor

Find some peace and quiet and listen to yourself – consistently

Isn't it amazing the wisdom that each of us holds and can access when we just get quiet?! Mama's intuition is powerful, powerful stuff.

~ Renee Trudeau, *Courageous Parents, Confident Kids* contributor

I love hearing that other moms are trusting their guts too. I remember reading Dr. Sears' book about birthing and his advice that we as moms know best. I think it's so true and have held onto those words for years (but I thought I was alone in flying by the seat of my pants).

∿ Amie Adams, TheMotherhood.com member

On any given day, any mom can find a study to tell her why she's doing a bad job. I believe that love covers a multitude of sins. We don't expect perfection from our children, our spouses, or our bosses. We can't beat ourselves up for not being perfect. Sometimes it's necessary to tune the media out so you can hear your own voice.

∿ Becki, TheMotherhood.com member

Get perspective – so you don't create your own version of reality
Don't you all feel like you have to tune the news out when it comes to parenting "studies" or stories? I feel like we have to rely on our gut or our [real life] or online communities for the real facts.

∿ Amie Adams, The Motherhood.com member

Without support, it's too easy to create your own reality and run with it – in a bad way. The support of other women and other moms offers, among other things, perspective. I know I'm not a bad mom, but it can be so reassuring to have another trusted woman tell me so on the days that I don't trust myself.

∿ Becki, TheMotherhood.com member

Be your own best mother, and pat yourself on the back for the progress you make

Is there really any woman who thinks she's the perfect parent? We all need to be gentle with ourselves and each other and remember that.

~ Amie Adams, TheMotherhood.com member

Amen, Amie. We only get one shot at parenting each child, and we need to give ourselves a break, find some peace, and create a frame of reference – a touchstone that can bring us back to center when life inevitably gets crazy again.

For us, that touchstone is moms online. We can't imagine life without them and the strength and encouragement they give us.

A couple of generations ago, our grandmothers and great-aunts gathered around the kitchen table to problem solve and be there for each other. In the same spirit of passing on advice, sharing war stories, building morale, and offering a shoulder to cry on – in a 21st century, social media way – we're meeting each other online and feeling stronger and more courageous for it.

We passionately believe that nothing is impossible when mothers in concert listen to their hearts and find the courage to make life a little better every day for themselves and each other.

We've lived it and are grateful every day.

Editor's Acknowledgments

Courageous Parents, Confident Kids is the result of a dedicated collaboration between the chapter contributors and the editorial team. To these amazing writers, I offer you my deepest thanks for not only believing in this project, but for making the concerted effort required to participate in it. You have brought important ideas to life and created a resource that will help families customize their own paths.

I hope this book will be the catalyst for an ongoing conversation that I intend to continue through my outreach online at MojoMom.com. In addition to blog updates and podcast interviews, I have several other new offerings in development, which I will announce through my MojoMom.com e-newsletter.

The chapter contributors all have amazing resources and expertise of their own to share, and I encourage all readers to explore the Web sites listed in each chapter contributor's biography, collected in the next section.

Special thanks go to the people who worked behind the scenes to make this book possible:

Lacey Mamak, our intrepid content editor, who has one of the sharpest minds I have encountered in my years of writing and teaching.

Patty Ayers of Ayers Virtual, project manager, who combines efficacy at work with adventure in life as well as anyone I know. Your example is inspiring!

The *Courageous Parents, Confident Kids* design team, which includes the brilliant cover-design firm Dunn + Associates Design, cover illustrator Jane Mjølsness, copywriter Susan Kendrick of Write To Your Market, and interior designer Dorie McClelland of Spring Book Design.

And finally, on behalf of all the contributors, gratitude to our families, who benefit from having a writer in the family on some days, and put up with it on others. We appreciate your patience, love and support!

About the Contributors

Renee Peterson Trudeau is a life balance and career coach, speaker, and the author of *The Mother's Guide to Self-Renewal: How to Reclaim, Rejuvenate and Re-Balance Your Life*, which provided the foundation for this chapter. Thousands of women around the globe are joining or becoming trained to lead Personal Renewal Groups (PRGs) using the *Guide*. Trudeau encourages all women to "find their tribe," whether that is through one of the hundreds of Personal Renewal Groups meeting worldwide or another women's circle. Learn more about PRGs, retreats, coaching, and life balance resources at www.ReneeTrudeau.com.

Kella Hatcher and Maryanne Perrin are the founders of Balancing Professionals, LLC. Through their research, writing, training, and consulting, they seek to redefine work by promoting workplace flexibility as a savvy strategy that benefits employers, employees, the community, and the environment. They are also the authors of *The On-Ramping Guide: Tips, Exercises, and Important Job Search Steps for Returning to Work After Time Out Raising Kids*. You can learn more about their work and access additional resources at www.BalancingProfessionals.com.

Maya Frost is an American writer, mindfulness trainer, and international lifestyle design consultant living in Argentina and Uruguay. She is the mother of four recently launched daughters and the author of *The New Global Student: Skip the SAT, Save Thousands on Tuition, and Get a Truly International Education.* Learn more at www.MayaFrost.com.

Melissa Stanton is the author of *The Stay-at-Home Survival Guide: Field-tested Strategies for Staying Smart, Sane, and Connected While Caring for Your Kids.* Prior to becoming a stay-at-home mother of three (including twins) in a suburb of Washington D.C., Melissa was a senior editor at *LIFE* and *People* magazines in New York. Her articles have appeared in *The New York Times, Glamour,* and *Brain,Child,* among other publications and Web sites. Having returned to the "work outside the home" workforce, Melissa is preparing a guide for at-home moms seeking paid employment. Visit with Melissa at www.RealLifeSupportForMoms.com.

Amy McCready is a parenting coach and the founder of Positive Parenting Solutions. Her online course empowers parents with the skills to permanently correct misbehaviors without nagging, reminding, or yelling. You can learn more about her training at www.PositiveParentingSolutions.com.

Jamie Woolf has a master's degree in industrial/organizational psychology and over 25 years of experience providing consulting to business leaders. Based on her work inside dozens of organizations, she founded The Parent Leader, a firm that conducts workshops to help parents combine self-awareness and leadership skills to transform their daily parenting challenges into desired results. Jamie is also the author of *Mom-in-Chief: How Wisdom from the Workplace Can Save Your Family from Chaos* and the co-founder of Pinehurst Consulting, an organization development consulting firm. She lives in Oakland, California with her husband and two daughters. To learn more about The Parent Leader's services and resources, visit www.MomInChief.com.

Irene van der Zande is the Executive Director and co-founder of Kidpower Teenpower Fullpower International, a nonprofit organization that has brought personal safety and confidence skills to over a million children, teens, and adults of many cultures across the United States and around the world. Since 1989, Irene has led the creation of the organization's curriculum, development of centers, and training of instructors, and has written extensively about personal safety. Irene is also the author of *1,2,3 . . . The Toddler Years* and co-author of the textbook *The Parent/Toddler Group*. To learn more about Kidpower's free articles, podcasts, and videos, as well as workshops, *Kidpower Safety Comics* and other print publications available for purchase, visit www.kidpower.org.

Linda Criddle is a 13-year Microsoft veteran and internationally recognized leader in Internet safety and technology. She is President of LOOK**BOTH**WAYS Inc., which develops cutting-edge safety software and provides consultation to the online industry, governments, law enforcement, and educators. Linda is also President of the LOOK**BOTH**WAYS Foundation, a nonprofit organization dedicated to bringing Internet curriculum to schools and educational materials to consumers of all ages. Linda is the author of *Look Both Ways: Help Protect Your Family on the Internet* and *Using the Internet Safely for Seniors for Dummies*. Linda also serves as the President of the Safe Internet Alliance, an advocacy group dedicated to bringing a safer online experience to all consumers. For more information about Internet safety or to contact Linda, go to www.iLookBothWays.com.

Joanne Bamberger is a recovering attorney, journalist, politically progressive mom, and political analyst living in the shadow of the nation's capital. Known around the blogosphere as "PunditMom," in addition to writing her own op-ed commentary blog, Joanne is a regular contributor to many news outlets, including *The Huffington Post* and *MOMocrats*. She is a former Contributing Editor at *BlogHer*, and a member of the inaugural class of the Progressive Women's Voices program at the Women's Media Center. Joanne's book, *Mothers of Intention*, based on her blog feature of the same name, will be published in the fall of 2010. Catch up with Joanne at www.PunditMom.com.

Kristin Rowe-Finkbeiner is Executive Director and co-founder of MomsRising.org, an online and on-the-ground grassroots organization of more than a million people who are working to achieve economic security for all families in the United States and to end discrimination against mothers. With MomsRising co-founder and President, Joan Blades, Kristin co-authored *The Motherhood Manifesto*. She also wrote the award-winning book *The F-Word: Feminism in Jeopardy*. In 2006, she was given an Excellence in Journalism award by the Society of Professional Journalists for magazine writing. Kristin has been deeply involved in cutting-edge politics, policy analysis, and grassroots organization for nearly two decades.

Cooper Munroe and Emily McKhann are the founding mothers of the web community for moms, TheMotherhood.com, and have been friends and colleagues for over 20 years. The seeds for TheMotherhood were planted after they experienced the power of moms online first-hand when they created a grassroots, person-to-person effort that delivered supplies to the Gulf Coast after Hurricane Katrina. Cooper and Emily are long-time members of the mothers' online community and have received the Best of Blogs Award for Most Inspirational Blog, a WebAward, and were a finalist in for a Webby Award. In 2010 they were named by *Parents Magazine* to the "Top Ten List of Power Moms Online."

About the Editor

Amy Tiemann, Ph.D., is a multi-media producer and educator who plays a central role in today's parenting conversation. *Courageous Parents, Confident Kids: Letting Go So You Both Can Grow* is the latest culmination of that expertise. Amy took on a unique leadership role in the parenting field with the creation of this book. Editor, collaborator, and catalyst for social change, she brought this group of outstanding experts together for the first time in one place. The result is this powerful new resource that guides parents on their family journeys *and* facilitates a dramatic shift in our cultural landscape.

Amy Tiemann's previous book, *Mojo Mom: Nurturing Your Self While Raising a Family,* now in its second edition, catapulted her MojoMom.com movement into what is now one of the most popular online parenting resources. Visitors have logged more than 90,000 downloads of her *Mojo Mom Podcasts* alone. A sought-after speaker and commentator, she is a frequent guest expert on parenting Web sites, national radio tours, magazines from *Redbook* to *Glamour*, and TV including NBC's *Today Show*. Tiemann received her Ph.D. in Neurosciences from Stanford University.

Made in the USA
San Bernardino, CA
07 March 2013